The Ironside Commentary Sei

STUDIES ON BOOK ON

PSALMS

By
H. A. IRONSIDE, Litt.D.

Author of NOTES ON JEREMIAH; LECTURES ON DANIEL;
NOTES ON EZRA, NEHEMIAH AND ESTHER; NOTES ON PROVERBS;
NOTES ON THE MINOR PROPHETS, etc., etc.

LOIZEAUX BROTHERS, Inc.
NEPTUNE, NEW JERSEY

Hope. Inspiration. Trust.

WE'RE SOCIAL! FOLLOW US FOR NEW TITLES AND DEALS:
FACEBOOK.COM/CROSSREACHPUBLICATIONS
@CROSSREACHPUB

AVAILABLE IN PAPERBACK AND EBOOK EDITIONS
PLEASE GO ONLINE FOR MORE GREAT TITLES
AVAILABLE THROUGH CROSSREACH PUBLICATIONS.
AND IF YOU ENJOYED THIS BOOK PLEASE CONSIDER LEAVING A
REVIEW ON AMAZON. THAT HELPS US OUT A LOT. THANKS.

CONTENTS

PREFACE

*I have fought a good fight, I have
finished my course, I have kept the
faith: Henceforth there is laid up
for me a crown of righteousness,
which the Lord, the righteous judge,
shall give me at that day: and not to me
only, but unto all them also that love
His appearing.*

2 TIMOTHY 4:7, 8

Harry A. Ironside is now at home with the Lord his Saviour, whom he deeply loved and so devotedly served.

The publishers are conscious of their deep privilege in preserving in book form these studies on the first book of the Psalms.

These addresses were originally given by Dr. Ironside at the *Moody Memorial Church* in Chicago, Illinois, and Printed in the Moody Church News. They are now reproduced in the earnest hope that they will be a means of rich blessing "unto all them also that love His appearing."

THE PUBLISHERS

New York
December 1951

INTRODUCTORY ADDRESS AND EXPOSITION OF PSALM 1

AS WE ARE ABOUT TO ENTER UPON THE STUDY OF THIS book, I want to say first a few things of an introductory character. I suppose there is no portion of Holy Scripture that has meant more to the people of God, particularly to tried and afflicted believers down through both the Jewish and Christian centuries, than the book of Psalms. Of course the worship expressed in this book does not rise to the full character of Christian worship as in this present dispensation of the grace of God.

As we read the Psalms we need to remember that when they were written our Lord Jesus had not yet become incarnate; consequently, redemption had not been effected, and so the veil was still unrent. God, as it were, was shut away from man, and man was shut out from God; and so the worshiper of Old Testament times gives expression to certain things that would not be suitable from the lips of an instructed worshiper in this present age of grace.

David prays, "Take not Thy Holy Spirit from me." No well instructed Christian would pray that today, for we know now that we have received the Holy Spirit to abide with us forever. We have been sealed by the Holy Spirit until the redemption of the purchased possession. And then there are a great many of the prayers in the book of Psalms that imply a hidden God. But today God has come out into the light, since our Lord Jesus, by His sacrificial death upon the Cross, has rent the veil and opened up the way into the immediate presence of God for poor sinners and enabled God to come out to man in all the perfection of His glorious Person.

There are some churches, and I do not speak now in any critical sense, that use the book of Psalms as the expression of their prayers and praise. Because this book is inspired they think of it as far superior, as a vehicle of prayer and praise, to any compilation of hymns or sacred songs written by uninspired men. But I am sure they are mistaken as to that, for since the coming of the Holy Spirit He has opened up truth to His people in this dispensation of grace that was utterly unknown to those in the days when the Psalms were written. But granting all that, we find a great deal that is precious and a great deal that is wonderfully helpful to feed the soul and uplift the spirit as we study these Old Testament Psalms.

It is a new thought to some people that we have not only one book of Psalms, but in reality there are five books. Our Bible begins with the Pentateuch, from Genesis to Deuteronomy; and the entire Bible, it has been pointed out by others, seems to be built upon that Pentateuchal foundation.

The book of Genesis is the book of life and the book of election; the book of Exodus is the book of redemption; Leviticus is the book of sanctification; Numbers is the book of testing and experience; Deuteronomy is the book of divine government. It is a very interesting fact that the book of Psalms consists of five books also and that these five link perfectly with the five books of Moses. The first book of the Psalms is from Psalm 1 through 41, and you will notice how Psalm 41, verse 13, concludes the first book: "Blessed be the Lord God of Israel from everlasting, and to everlasting. Amen, and Amen." The second book begins with Psalm 42 and goes on through Psalm 72. Notice how this book ends, Psalm 72:18–20: "Blessed be the Lord God, the God of Israel, who only doeth wondrous things. And blessed be His glorious name for ever: and let the whole earth be filled with His glory; Amen, and Amen. The prayers of David the son of Jesse are ended." Then the third book comprises Psalms 73 to 89 and ends, Psalm 89:52, with the words: "Blessed be the Lord for evermore. Amen, and Amen." The fourth book includes Psalms 90 to 106. Look at the closing verse of this book, Psalm 106:48: "Blessed be the Lord God of Israel from everlasting to everlasting: and let all the people say, Amen. Praise ye the Lord." And the fifth book is from Psalm 107 to 150, and you know how that winds up, verse 6: "Let every thing that hath breath praise the Lord. Praise ye the Lord."

The doxologies that close each of the books (and you do not find them anywhere else in the Psalms) enable us to distinguish them clearly. We have a progressive line of truth in accord with the subjects treated in the five books of the Pentateuch, and the remarkable thing is that in the first book of Psalms the great outstanding themes are, Divine Life and Electing Grace—God's wonderful provision of grace, just the same as in the book of Genesis. In the second book of Psalms the great outstanding theme is Redemption, as in Exodus. And in the third book of Psalms we are occupied with Sanctification, communion with God, the way into the sanctuary, as in the book of Leviticus. The fourth book is the darkest one, for it is the book of testing, the book of trial, as in Numbers. Many of these Psalms have to do with bitter, hard experiences that the people of God often have to go through in this world. And then the last book of Psalms is the book that brings God in as overruling in all the trials, the difficulties, and perplexities—the divine government, as in the book of Deuteronomy—God bringing everything out at last to His honor and glory and to His people's eternal blessing.

I do not know how anybody could get any conception of the remarkable design of the Word of God, of which I have just given you a little intimation, and question for one moment its divine inspiration. Only God could have given this wonderful order. While the books of the Pentateuch were all written by one man, Moses, the books of the Psalms were written by many men. We call this book ordinarily, "the Psalms of David," but David did not write them all. A great many of them were written by other people. They were the Psalms of David in the sense that we call the old gospel hymn book, "The Moody and Sankey Hymn Book." Moody did not write any of the hymns and Sankey only a sprinkling of them, but these men compiled the book. If you go over to Great Britain today you can go to the original publishers of it and say, "I would like to have a copy of the Moody and Sankey Hymn Book," and they will hand you a book with twelve hundred hymns in it. In the old days this book had only about six hundred hymns. It was compiled by them originally, but a great many others have been added from time to time, and today there is this vast collection. We can think of the book of the Psalms of David in the same way. It was he in the first place who compiled this book, and it was a kind of hymn book in the temple worship. Doubtless many of these were used before the temple was built, when David brought the ark of the covenant to Jerusalem and built a special sanctuary for it. But after David passed away, Solomon added more Psalms to the book, perhaps largely through the direction of Ethan and Asaph and several others who were singers in the temple choir after that glorious sanctuary had been built by King Solomon.

In all probability two Psalms in this wonderful little book claim Moses as the author. If you turn to the ninetieth Psalm you will see at the heading, "A Prayer of Moses the man of God"; while the ninety-first Psalm has no heading at all. The reason is this: according to the Jewish authorities, originally Psalms 90 and 91 were one, but later on for convenience' sake, just as we sometimes cut our long hymns into two, this long Psalm was cut into two; and in Psalm 90 we have the first man, and in 91 the Second Man. But in all probability it was all written by Moses.

Several of the Psalms seem to have been written by King Solomon. We are told that Solomon wrote a great many songs. We have in our Bible the Canticles, "The song of songs, which is Solomon's" (Song of Solomon 1:1). But we also have one or two Psalms that bear his name. And then there are other Psalms by different writers which we will notice as we go on.

It would seem as though some of the Psalms could not have been written until after the people returned from Babylon. You will remember the Psalm that says, "By the rivers of Babylon, there we sat down, yea, we wept, when we remembered Zion. We hanged our harps upon the willows in the midst thereof. For there they that carried us away captive required of us a song; and they that wasted us required of us mirth, saying, Sing us one of the songs of Zion. How shall we sing the Lord's song in a strange land?" (Psa. 137:1–4). It is not likely that David wrote this, but it was evidently written after the people had been carried to Babylon, and when they returned to their land it was added to the book. We shall find as we go on that there are some very interesting lessons to be gleaned from the settings of these various Psalms.

PSALM 1

The first Psalm is the inspired introduction to the entire book. We may say that we have here, in contrast, two men, the blessed man and the wicked man. The blessed man is the Second Man, the Lord from heaven; the wicked man is the first man.

Notice the opening verses. "Blessed is the man that walketh not in the counsel of the ungodly, nor standeth in the way of sinners, nor sitteth in the seat of the scornful. But his delight is in the law of the Lord; and in His law doth he meditate day and night. And he shall be like a tree planted by the rivers of water, that bringeth forth his fruit in his season; his leaf also shall not wither; and whatsoever he doeth shall prosper."

Who is this blessed man to whom our attention is directed as we open this lovely Old Testament book of praise and prayer? Observe in the first place that the tenses as we have them here do not exactly convey the thought of the original Hebrew. It may be rendered, "Blessed is the man that *hath not* walked in the counsel of the ungodly, nor *stood* in the way of sinners, nor *sat* in the seat of the scornful." He is not here expressing the blessedness of a man who was once a sinner and has been turned to righteousness and now no longer walks in the counsel of the ungodly, nor stands in the way of sinners, nor sits in the seat of the scornful. But he is telling us of the blessedness of the Man who has never done any of these things, the Man who never took his own way, the Man who never walked with the world as part of it, who never did a thing in opposition to the will of God. Who is that man?

I was very much impressed, a number of years ago, listening to Joseph Flacks tell of his visit to Palestine. When he was in the city of Jerusalem he was given the opportunity of addressing quite a gathering of Jews and Arabs. They were presumably unconverted. He took for his text this first Psalm. Of course he could repeat it to them in their own language, in the Hebrew. He dwelt upon the tenses as I have given them to you, "Blessed is the man who *hath not* walked in the counsel of the ungodly, nor *stood* in the way of sinners, nor *sat* in the seat of the scornful," and he said to them, "Now my brethren, who is this blessed Man of whom the Psalmist speaks? Notice this happy Man is a man who never walked in the counsel of the ungodly; He never stood in the way of sinners; He never sat in the seat of the scornful. He was an absolutely sinless Man. Who is this blessed Man?" Nobody spoke, and Joseph Flacks said, "Shall we say He is our great Father Abraham? Is it Father Abraham that the Psalmist is speaking of here?"

One old Jew said, "No, no; it cannot be Abraham, for he denied his wife; he told a lie about her."

"Ah," said Joseph Flacks, "it does not fit, does it? Abraham, although he was the father of the faithful, yet was a sinner who had to be justified by faith. But, my brethren, this refers to somebody; who is this Man? Could it be our great law giver, Moses?"

"No, no," they said, "it cannot be Moses. He killed a man and hid him in the sand." And another said, "And he lost his temper by the water of Meribah."

"Well," Joseph Flacks said, "my brethren, who is it? There is some Man here that the Spirit of God is bringing before us. Could it be our great King David, the sweet Psalmist of Israel who perhaps wrote this Psalm?"

"No, no," they cried, "it cannot be David. He committed adultery and had Uriah slain."

"Well," he said, "who is it; to whom do these words refer?"

They were quiet for some little time, and then one Jew arose and said, "My brethren, I have a little book here; it is called the New Testament. I have been reading it. If I believe this book, if I could be sure that it is true, I would say the Man of the first Psalm was Jesus of Nazareth."

An old Jew got right up and said, "My brethren, the Man of the first Psalm is Jesus of Nazareth. He is the only One who ever went through this world who never walked in the counsel of the ungodly nor stood in the way of sinners." And then this old man told how he had been brought to believe in Christ, and he took that occasion to openly confess his faith. He had been searching for a long time and had found out some time before that Jesus was the One, but he had not had the courage to tell others.

Ah yes, there is only one Man who ever walked through this scene to whom these words apply. The One of whom David speaks here is the One who hung on Calvary's cross, and who in the words of the twenty-second Psalm cried, "My God, My God, why hast Thou forsaken Me?" (Psa. 22:1).

How delightful it is to contemplate Him, to think of Him coming down into the world His hands had made, becoming man and going through this scene in all perfection, ministering to the needs of sinners but never joining with them in their rebellion against the Father.

"But His delight is in the law of the Lord; and in His law doth He meditate day and night." You remember that verse in the book of the Prophet Isaiah where he is speaking of what is said of God the Father: "He wakeneth morning by morning, He wakeneth mine ear to hear as the learned" (Isa. 50:4). God was daily communing with His blessed Son, and the Son was daily communing with the Father; and as He meditated on the Word of God, He was drawing from the Word, as man, the strength and the knowledge that was to enable Him to fulfill His divine mission. When you think of God's Holy Son feeding on the Word, delighting in the Word, and then think how little you and I, who need it so much, delight in it, it is enough to humble us before Him. These words of the first Psalm were true of our blessed Lord, and in measure will be of us as we meditate on His Word day and night.

"And He shall be like a tree planted by the rivers of water, that bringeth forth His fruit in His season; His leaf also shall not wither; and whatsoever He doeth shall prosper." Young people starting out in life are eager to make a success of life. They would like to prosper, they would like to do well. Here is the secret of successful living, the secret of prosperity; it is found in the first chapter of the book of Joshua, verse 8: "This book of the law shall not depart out of thy mouth; but thou shalt meditate therein day and night, that thou mayest observe to do according to all that is written therein: for then thou shalt make thy way prosperous, and then thou shalt have good success." That is what made the way of the Lord Jesus prosperous, and that will make your way prosperous—feeding upon the Word.

Now look at the contrast between Christ and every other man by nature. Verses 4, 5, and 6: "The ungodly are not so"—they may seem to prosper; they may seem to do better in this world than the righteous; they may get more, may lay up more money perhaps because they can use methods to make money that the righteous man cannot. "Men will praise thee," we are told, "when thou doest well to thyself" (Psa. 49:18). But it is one thing to have the praise of men and another to have the praise of God. "But are like the chaff which the wind driveth away. Therefore the ungodly shall not stand in the judgment, nor sinners in the congregation of the righteous." What does it mean to stand in the judgment? It means to be justified before God. We read in Romans of "this grace wherein we *stand*" (Rom. 5:2). The believer in the Lord Jesus Christ stands before God in all the infinite value of the finished work of our blessed Saviour, and no charge can be brought against him. Yes, men may seem now to prosper; they may seem now to get on well, but in that coming day when all things shall be opened up before the eyes of a Holy God they will shrink away from His presence in terror as they cry, "The great day of His wrath is come; and who shall be able to *stand?*" (Rev. 6:17). It is a great thing to be able to stand. It is a great thing to be able to say, "Thank God, my standing is in the risen Christ! I claim nothing on the ground of my own merit but stand before God in His perfection."

And now the last verse, "For the Lord knoweth the way of the righteous: but the way of the ungodly shall perish." And as you go on through the book of Psalms, as also in Proverbs, you will find these two ways contrasted throughout. In Psalm after Psalm the way of the righteous, the way that pleases God, the way that glorifies Him is contrasted with the way of the ungodly, the way of those who forget God, who turn away from Him, refuse subjection to His holy will.

THE SECOND PSALM

THE BOOK OF PSALMS HAS A VERY WONDERFUL PROPHETIC character. It sets forth in a most marvelous way the counsels of God in relation to the earth, and the efforts of Satan to thwart those counsels. In the first book, Psalms 1 to 41, we see the conflict raging between God and the forces of evil, a conflict that begins with the coming of the Lord Jesus Christ into this world, that centers in the Cross, and then after the resurrection of Christ goes right on until His second coming. All the experiences, also, that His people pass through as associated with the rejected Christ come before us very vividly in this first book of the Psalms.

The second book of Psalms, 42 to 72, shows us that God's counsels are going to be carried out in spite of all the efforts of Satan to hinder, and we see the people of God, the nation of Israel, scattered among the Gentiles and suffering terribly, as they have been all down through the centuries since the rejection of Christ.

Then when we come to the third book, Psalms 73 to 89, we see the remnant of Israel in the land of Palestine after they have been gathered out from the nations of the Gentiles, waiting for the Messiah but suffering terribly under the persecution of the beast and the antichrist. Their suffering comes to a climax in Psalm 88, where they cry out in anguish as the waves and billows of judgment roll over them just before the blessed Lord appears in grace for their glorious deliverance, as shown in Psalm 89, when the King, great David's greater Son, comes to take the kingdom and delivers His people.

In the fourth book we see Messiah reigning in Zion, and the first man with all the sin and sorrow and wretchedness that he has brought into the world displaced, and God's Second Man, the Lord from heaven, bringing in millennial blessing.

In the fifth book, 107 to 150, we have the celebration of the divine government, everything that has breath called upon to bless and glorify God because of the marvelous way in which at last righteousness has triumphed over evil; light has displaced darkness, and the blessed Lord Jesus Christ is reigning with every foe beneath His feet.

This gives us the prophetic outline of the book of Psalms, and it is a wonderful thing, as we read this Old Testament hymn book—for that is really what it is—to see the orderly way in which one Psalm follows another. If anybody has any doubt as to the divine inspiration of Scripture, it seems to me that a careful study of the book of Psalms alone ought to make clear to him that God has ordered all these things, even to the arrangement of this wonderful book. In our hymn books we have a beautiful collection of gospel lyrics and sweet and sacred hymns, but we could displace them; we could take them all, if we had the plates, and mix them up and then put them together again, and it would make very little difference. But if you were to change the position of one of these Psalms, you would dislocate the entire thing. Every Psalm is found in the exact place where God would have it in order to tell the story in a smooth, orderly way. But of course you need to have your eyes open to discern this. If you are thinking only of yourself as you read these Psalms you will never see what the book is really taking up, but once you understand something of God's prophetic counsel, once you enter into His purpose in Christ Jesus for the people of Israel and the Gentile nations, you will realize how marvelously this book fits in with the divine program.

We saw that in the first Psalm two men stand out in vivid contrast and that these two are the first Adam and the last Adam. When I speak of the first man, I do not mean Adam alone but Adam and his entire race, because Scripture recognizes only two men. The Bible is the history of two men. In 1 Corinthians 15:47 we are told, "The first man is of the earth, earthy: the Second Man is the Lord from heaven." Who was that first man? Well, you say, That is Adam. Very well, the Second Man is who? Cain? No. But was he not the second man? Yes, he was the second man to appear on earth, but as God looked at him he was only another edition of the first man, and every man born into the world since has been just another copy of the first man. It is just like an edition of a book. You might have 50,000 copies but they are all just the same book, and so you can have millions and billions of men who have been born into this world, but they are all just copies of the first man. Adam begat a son in his own image and after his own likeness, and every one coming into the world since has borne the image and the likeness of Adam. And so Scripture says that the first man, taking in the whole human race, "is of the earth, earthy." And then it says, "The Second Man is the Lord from heaven." And the moment poor sinners put their trust in Jesus they are linked with the Second Man. He is their head, and the link with the first man is broken forever. So then you see Christ in contrast to the first man in Psalm 1.

In Psalm 2 we have Jehovah's determination to make Christ ruler over all things, to give Him the throne on Mount Zion and thus to make Him the Messiah expected by the people of Israel, who is to rule over all the Gentile world and bring in everlasting blessing. But when He comes into the world, it is not ready for Him, and you have the story told in a wonderful way in this Psalm.

It has been pointed out often that this Psalm consists of twelve verses, is divided into four sections of three verses each, and in each section there is a different speaker, so that in this second Psalm you listen to four different voices. Whose voices are they?

In the first three verses you have the voice of the world. Listen to it, "Why do the heathen [the Gentile nations] rage, and the people [the Jewish nation] imagine a vain thing?" "The people" is the term applied to Israel. "The nations" refers to the Gentiles. "The kings of the earth [that is, the kings of the Gentiles] set themselves, and the rulers [the rulers of the Jews] take counsel together, against the Lord, and against His anointed." And now Jews and Gentiles, acting through their respective leaders, express the voice of the whole world, the attitude of the entire world toward God. God hath set forth Christ to be the King, to bring in blessing for Jews and Gentiles. What is the answer to the love of God's heart in sending Christ? Listen to the voice of the world, verse 3: "Let us break their bands asunder, and cast away their cords from us." That is what man says. We do not want to be subjected to God; we do not want God's King; we do not want His millennium; we do not want to be subject to His righteous rule. They said that when the Lord was here on earth, "We have no king but Caesar" (John 19:15). In other words, we are not for this Man; we will not have Him to reign over us.

As recorded in the fourth chapter of Acts we find that the apostles, immediately after Pentecost, came up against this and recognized that the second Psalm was being fulfilled even then. They were having a prayer meeting; they were talking to God. Read Acts 4 beginning with verse 24: "When they heard that, they lifted up their voice to God with one accord, and said, Lord, Thou art God, which hast made heaven, and earth, and the sea, and all that in them is: Who by the mouth of Thy servant David hast said, Why did the heathen rage, and the people imagine vain things?" And then they applied it, "The kings of the earth stood up [that is, the Gentile rulers], and the rulers were gathered together [that is, the heads of the Jewish people] against the Lord, and against His Christ. For of a truth against Thy holy Child Jesus, whom Thou hast anointed, both Herod, and Pontius Pilate, with the Gentiles, and the people of Israel, were gathered together." Herod represented the Jews. He was the king of the Jewish nation though a half Edomite himself. Pilate represented the empire yonder at Rome. And then those high priests and leaders of Israel lifted their voices up against God and His Son, the Lord Jesus Christ.

But notice, they could go only as far as God in His sovereignty permitted them to go. "The Gentiles, and the people of Israel, were gathered together, For to do whatsoever Thy hand and Thy counsel determined before to be done." They could not go one step beyond His definite permission. God did allow them to crucify His Son, to nail Him to a tree, to seal His body up in a tomb, but that was as far as they could go. Then what happened? Turn back to the second Psalm. Man now has done his worst; man has shown out all the bitter hatred and malignity in his heart toward God and Christ. He could not do anything worse than crucify the Lord of Glory.

Now listen to another voice, verses 4 to 6, "He that sitteth in the heavens shall laugh: the Lord shall have them in derision." They think they are having their own way, but God looks on in derision; He sees the end from the beginning. "Then shall He speak unto them in His wrath, and vex them in His sore displeasure." And now you hear the second voice. It is the voice of God, the Father, and what does He say? "Yet have I set My King upon My holy hill of Zion." They thought they had gotten rid of Him. They said, "We have no king but Caesar"; they cried, "Crucify Him, crucify Him," and their will was carried out and His precious dead body sealed up in Joseph's tomb; but God had not changed His mind. He is to reign in Zion yet. He is going to have the throne just as surely as He had the cross.

"Yet have I set My King upon My holy hill of Zion." He is looking on to the day of His return, to the day when the Lord Jesus will come back from the glory to which He has gone, and His feet shall stand again upon the Mount of Olives, and He will enter into the city of Zion and reign gloriously there before His ancients. Some of us believe that the day is drawing very, very near when this Scripture is going to have its marvelous fulfillment, when the world again will see the Lord Jesus Christ, for it is written, "Behold, He cometh with clouds; and every eye shall see Him, and they also which pierced Him: and all kindreds of the earth shall wail because of Him" (Rev. 1:7).

In the next three verses we have another voice, that of the Son of God, the rejected Messiah. It is as though He is meditating on what the Father has said to Him. He is speaking out loud in order that you and I may hear what is going on in His mind. Verse 7: "I will declare the decree: the Lord hath said unto Me, Thou art My Son; this day have I begotten Thee." That is, God is saying to the Lord Jesus Christ, "Whatever men may do does not change your relationship to Me. You are My Son, My begotten Son." Of course, the begetting here refers to His coming into the world. He was begotten of the Holy Spirit in the womb of the Virgin Mary. God says of Him, You are My begotten Son and I am going to carry out the plans by reason of which I sent You into the world.

"Ask of Me, and I shall give Thee the heathen [the nations] for Thine inheritance, and the uttermost parts of the earth for Thy possession." It is as though the Father says to Him, Your own people did not want You; the people of Israel rejected You, but I have something greater for You than to be accepted only by Israel. Ask of Me and I will give You a great inheritance, a great ingathering from the heathen world. "Ask of Me, and I shall give Thee the heathen for Thine inheritance, and the uttermost parts of the earth for Thy possession. Thou shalt break them with a rod of iron; Thou shalt dash them in pieces like a potter's vessel." That is, they are to be broken down by Messiah's power, broken down before God in repentance and brought to accept and to own Him as the righteous Lord and Saviour. In a wonderful way this is going on even now. It is going to have its fulfillment in the millennial days when the nations everywhere will be brought to recognize the authority of the Lord Jesus Christ. I never come to a missionary meeting but I feel as though there ought to be written right across the entire platform, "Ask of Me, and I shall give Thee the heathen for Thine inheritance, and the uttermost parts of the earth for Thy possession." It is the will of God that His Son should have a great heritage out of the heathen world, the godless Gentiles.

But now we come to the closing part of this Psalm, and in the last three verses we listen to another voice, a very gentle, a very loving, a very tender voice. I hope you have heard it. If you have not, it is not because it has not called but because your ears have become so accustomed to the sounds of earth that they are not attuned to the voice of the Holy Spirit.

We have listened to the voice of the world, the voice of the Father, the voice of the Son, and now we hear the voice of the Holy Spirit of God. Verse 10: "Be wise now therefore, O ye kings: be instructed, ye judges of the earth." It is a call to all in authority everywhere to recognize the claims of the Son of God. "Serve the Lord with fear." That is, with reverence, with awe; not with dread, not as one to be afraid of, but reverential fear such as a dutiful son gives to his father or to his mother. "Serve the Lord with fear, and rejoice with trembling. Kiss the Son, lest He be angry, and ye perish from the way, when His wrath is kindled but a little." Do you get the beauty of that? Here is the rejected King and He appears before men now not as a mighty conqueror coming to smite down His enemies but in all the majesty of His kingly authority. He reaches out a hand and as you look at it, there is a scar, for it is the hand that was once nailed to a cross. He holds out the hand of peace, and the Holy Spirit says, "Poor rebellious sinners, do not fight against Him; do not wait until the day when the wrath of the Lamb shall come, but now bow at His feet, kiss the Son, kiss that wounded hand in token that you surrender to Him, that you refuse any longer to fight against Him, to associate yourself with the world that is rejecting Him." This is the day of His mercy. In that day of wrath it will be too late and you will perish from the way.

> "The hands of Christ seem very frail,
> For they were broken by a nail,
> But only they reach heaven
> Whom those frail, broken hands hold fast."

Have you ever kissed the Son? Have you ever bowed at His feet, surrendering to Him?

Look at these last words: "Blessed are all they that put their trust in Him." And that is the message going out to the whole world and that will continue until the day of His wrath. What a wonderful thing to be able to say, "I am trusting Thee, Lord Jesus, trusting only Thee."

THE SUFFERING PEOPLE OF GOD

PSALMS 3, 4, AND 5

THE FIRST EIGHT PSALMS CONSTITUTE AN OCTAVE IN which all are intimately connected. We have already looked at Psalms 1 and 2, but now we want to link them with the six that follow. In this octave we have our Lord Jesus Christ presented to us as the Second Man, the only perfect Man who ever trod this earth. He, as we have already seen, is the blessed Man of Psalm 1, and He stands out in vivid contrast to the first man, to all who are linked with the first man, Adam, by natural birth, to the ungodly.

Then in Psalm 2 we have seen this Second Man presented by God as King to reign in Zion, and one might have thought, knowing how terribly distraught men were because of the crimes and wickedness and difficulty they had to face in all the nations, that they would gladly have opened their hearts to the true King when He came. But instead of that we find them saying, "We will not have this Man to reign over us" (Luke 19:14), and so the King was rejected, and with the rejection of the King we have the setting to one side of the kingdom. Some people imagine that the kingdom of God is now in force in this world, and we hear a great deal in many quarters about "building the kingdom," and our responsibility to build the kingdom; but the fact of the matter is that the kingdom as set forth in Scripture has never yet been set up in this world. It was presented to men when the Lord Jesus Christ was here, when He said, "The kingdom of God is among you" (Luke 17:21), not exactly, perhaps, as translated in our version, "The kingdom of God is *within* you." He was really saying to the people who were looking for the coming of the kingdom, "It is already among you"; that is, the King is here. There were His disciples gathered about Him, and they constituted His cabinet. He tells them that because they followed Him, in the regeneration, that is, in the making of all things new, they shall sit upon thrones judging the twelve tribes of Israel. They were the executors of His kingdom. As He stood with this group of apostles He could say, "You are looking for the kingdom? You are thinking of it as something yet to come? It is here because the King is here, and here are His loyal subjects." But in Pilate's judgment hall they cried, "We have no king but Caesar," and so refused and rejected God's anointed King. What has happened? He went to the Cross, settled the sin question, and now is like the nobleman pictured in Luke 19 who went into a far country to receive for himself a kingdom and to return, and in His absence we are not building the kingdom, but the Spirit of God is using those who love the Lord Jesus, those who seek to serve Him to call out from among the Gentiles and from Israel a people for His name. These people, when they are saved, when they trust the Lord Jesus, are constituted by the baptism of the Holy Spirit, the Church, the body of Christ; and when Christ returns to reign, His people will reign with Him. In the meantime His kingdom is set up in our hearts. That is, we who trust Him, we who love Him, recognize Him as the only rightful King though rejected by the world; and so in that sense we speak of the kingdom in its mystery form, hidden in the hearts of those who love Him.

During all this present waiting time, ere the King comes back and takes possession of the entire universe so that the kingdoms of the world shall actually become the kingdom of our Lord and of His Christ, His people have to suffer, have to know what it is to be misunderstood by the world, to endure persecution and trial and difficulty. Their Head is rejected, the true King is rejected, and so His saints are rejected with Him. We sing sometimes:

"Our Lord is now rejected and by the world disowned,
By the many still neglected and by the few enthroned,
But soon He'll come in glory, the hour is drawing nigh,
For the crowning day is coming by and by."

Until that day we cannot expect to be recognized by the world that cast out our Saviour; we cannot expect to feel at home in this scene where He had no home. But when He comes back, He will purge the world with righteous judgment, and then we shall reign with Him.

Those of us who are acquainted with New Testament truth know that when He comes, the first thing He will do will be to call His own redeemed people out of this scene to meet Him in the air. And then what? Will that be the end of His dealings with men down here? No; God never leaves Himself without witnesses; though there will come a moment when there will not be a Christian left in the world. The solemn thing is that it might take place tonight. This should not trouble us. It ought not to alarm the bride to know that the bridegroom may come for her at any time, if she is really in love with him. Our blessed Bridegroom whom we love may come at any moment, and there will not be one Christian left in the world. But will that be an end to God's mercy to mankind? No; because we learn from Scripture that "blindness in part is happened to Israel, until the fullness of the Gentiles be come in" (Rom. 11:25). Then God will turn again to the people of Israel and will draw the hearts of honest Israelites to search their own Scriptures; and as a result, light will break upon their souls, and so there will soon be found in this world a remnant people out of Israel who will be waiting, not for the Saviour to come in the air, for that will have already come to pass, but for the King to come to the earth with all His heavenly saints who have been caught up to meet Him, to establish His kingdom and reign in Mount Zion, as indicated in that second Psalm. And when He reigns He will reign not only over the nation of Israel but also over all the earth; and in view of that He takes a much wider title than "King in Zion." He calls Himself the "Son of Man." We read, "When the Son of Man shall come in His glory, and all the holy angels with Him," etc. (Matt. 25:31). He will take possession of the world, and at His revelation many will recognize Him as the true Saviour and King and will bow in obedience to Him. Those who refuse allegiance will be cut off in judgment. Those who bow at His feet will enter, not into heaven, but into the kingdom that is going to be set up here on earth.

During the interval between the taking of the saints to heaven and the coming back with the Lord when He returns to reign, the people of Israel who have turned to Him will have to suffer almost incredulous persecution. It will be the time of Jacob's trouble or, as the Lord Jesus calls it, the great tribulation, the time of distress "such as was not since the beginning of the world to this time, no, nor ever shall be." In fact He says, "And except those days should be shortened, there should no flesh be saved." But then we read, "Immediately after the tribulation of those days … they shall see the Son of Man coming in the clouds of heaven with power and great glory" (Matt. 24:21, 22, 29, 30).

In Psalm 1 you have the Second Man; in Psalm 2, the rejected King; and then in Psalms 3 to 7 you have the suffering and yet the confidence of the people of God in the interval until the Saviour returns again. When you come to Psalm 8 you have the glory of the Son of Man taking possession of the kingdom and ruling over the entire universe in righteousness: King in Psalm 2, Son of Man in Psalm 8, and so you can see how this is a connected series with everything in perfect order.

Let us look now at the third Psalm. It is interesting to notice the heading, "A Psalm of David, when he fled from Absalom his son." David, the true king, was rejected and Absalom, the usurper, was reigning; and that is the condition of things now. Our Lord Jesus, the true King, is rejected and an usurper is on the throne; so we can expect suffering and sorrow. David's experience pictures in a very wonderful way what the people of God will go through during the day of the Lord's rejection. And may I say that in all these Psalms, 3 to 7, we have set forth in a peculiar way the sufferings that the remnant of Israel will endure in the days of the great tribulation. But they also apply to God's people at any time while waiting for the coming again of the rejected King.

Let us read a part of Psalm 3, "Lord, how are they increased that trouble me! many are they that rise up against me. Many there be which say of my soul, There is no help for him in God." We might entitle this Psalm, "God the All-sufficient One." Here is the child of God in real distress because all around are enemies who are taunting him and threatening him and saying to him, "There is no help for you; you trust in a God your eyes have never seen; He cannot do anything for you; there is no help for you in God." The world says that now, but the people of God can look up and say, "But Thou, O Lord, art a shield for me; my glory, and the lifter up of mine head." No matter how dark the days, no matter how foes may rage around, no matter how dreadful Satan's malignancy may be, God Himself is our shield, and He is the One who lifts up our heads. So a saint of God can say, "I cried unto the Lord with my voice, and He heard me out of His holy hill." And yet that does not mean that he is delivered from trouble. David was fleeing from Absalom, and he was a wanderer in the wilderness while his foes were seeking him; yet he tells us in this Psalm how he was able to hand his case over to God. It is a great thing to be able to do that, to say, it is not a question now of my ability to stand against the foe; it is not a question of my ability to weather this trouble, my ability to overcome my enemies; but I am putting the whole thing into the hands of God and He stands between me and the foe.

Notice the perfect confidence expressed in the verses that follow, "I laid me down and slept; I awaked; for the Lord sustained me." Do you think you could have done that? Here is David fleeing from Absalom, not knowing what moment the army will be coming over the hill; but night has fallen, and he has committed himself to God, and so he wraps his robe around him and lies down and goes to sleep! He is safe, for he has handed everything over to God. "I laid me down and slept," and when morning comes, he says, "I awaked; for the Lord sustained me." In other words, I just had a real good sleep with all the foes seeking my destruction. It is only when you hand everything over to God that that can be possible. David says, "Lord, You know all about Absalom; You know all about my foes. They are determined to destroy me. You know how ungrateful my son Absalom is. Lord, You look after me." And in the morning if one had asked, "How did you sleep?" he could have said, "I had a fine sleep and I awaked; for the Lord sustained me."

And so, strong in faith he says, "I will not be afraid of ten thousands of people, that have set themselves against me round about" Why? Because, after all, the battle is not his; it is God's. So he turns to the Lord and says, "Arise, O Lord; save me, O my God"; and then in faith cries, though his eyes have not yet seen it, "for Thou hast smitten all mine enemies upon the cheek bone; Thou hast broken the teeth of the ungodly." You cannot do much biting if your teeth are broken. They were just like a lot of yelping hounds after David, but he sees them with broken teeth and, this, long before the battle was fought. When eventually the army of Absalom came against Joab and the army of David, and they were defeated, it was no more real to David than when he handed it over to God in the wilderness. What a wonderful thing to be able to rest in God like that and count on His infinite love and power. "Salvation belongeth unto the Lord: Thy blessing is upon Thy people."

In the next Psalm you have a continuation of the same spirit of trust and confidence. You might call Psalm 4, "Confidence in God." David turns to God as the God of righteousness, and knows he can depend upon him. "Hear me when I call, O God of my righteousness." Whatever righteousness I have I get from God. I have none of my own. "Thou hast enlarged me when I was in distress; have mercy upon me, and hear my prayer." And then he turns to the enemies around about, like the remnant of Israel as they see the power of antichrist and the beast seeking to destroy them. "O ye sons of men, how long will ye turn My glory into shame? how long will ye love vanity, and seek after leasing? But know that the Lord hath set apart him that is godly for Himself." Who is the godly man? The man that gives God the right place in his heart, and the Lord says, I have set that man apart for Myself. "The Lord will hear when I call unto Him."

Then follows the soul at rest, and David is just communing, as it were, with his own soul. He says, "Stand in awe, and sin not." Just wait quietly for God to act. "Commune with your own heart upon your bed, and be still. Offer the sacrifices of righteousness, and put your trust in the Lord." Notice the two things that are mentioned here, see that there is nothing wrong in your own life, and then you can put your trust in Him. If you are offering the sacrifices of unrighteousness, if there is wickedness and crookedness and unholiness in your life, it is no use talking about trusting God. "If I regard iniquity in my heart, the Lord will not hear me" (Psa. 66:18). But if I have judged everything that the Spirit of God has shown me to be wrong, I can offer the sacrifice of praise without a condemning conscience and can trust and not be afraid.

"There be many that say, Who will shew us any good?" David, you say the Lord is going to undertake? Let us see it He says, Lord, You answer—"Lord, lift Thou up the light of Thy countenance upon us. Thou hast put gladness in my heart, more than in the time that their corn and their wine increased." Men of this world are happy when things go well with them outwardly. We have often pointed out that there is a great difference between peace and happiness. Happiness depends upon the "haps." The old English word "hap" means a chance, and with the world if the "haps" are agreeable, if the chance events of life are satisfactory, then the worldling is happy, and if the "haps" are not satisfactory, he is un-happy. But with the Christian, whatever the "haps" are, if everything he has counted on goes to pieces, it does not make any difference. God is not going to pieces. God is there just the same, and so the soul can rest in Him. Therefore, even though a fugitive as David was, or a sufferer under the hand of antichrist as the remnant of Israel will be, the believer can say, "Thou hast put gladness in my heart." There is a settled peace there, "More than in the time that their corn and their wine increased." And so again the Psalmist says, "I will both lay me down in peace, and sleep." I will just leave it all with God and go to sleep. That is faith. "For Thou, Lord, only makest me dwell in safety." I can just trust Thee, I can leave it all with Thee. One has to learn to hand everything over to God, for we cannot undertake for ourselves or for our own in any power we possess. God alone can undertake for me.

In the fifth Psalm it is the holiness of God that is celebrated. And again we hear David lifting his voice in prayer, "Give ear to my words, O Lord, consider my meditation. Hearken unto the voice of my cry, my King, and my God: for unto thee will I pray. My voice shalt Thou hear in the morning, O Lord; in the morning will I direct my prayer unto Thee, and will look up." He was going to start the day aright. It is a great thing to do that. Did He hear your voice this morning? Did you start the day without any word with Him, and have you wondered why things went wrong today? They always will if you launch out on the work of the day without speaking to Him first. In the Song of Solomon the bridegroom says, "Let me hear thy voice, let me see thy countenance." And that is what our blessed Lord is saying to us—"I want you to take time to talk with Me, to read My Word and let Me speak to you through it. I want you to pour out your heart in prayer. I want to see your face and hear your voice." If you want to be a strong overcoming believer in a day of difficulty, be sure to start the day with God.

"For Thou art not a God that hath pleasure in wickedness: neither shall evil dwell with Thee. The foolish shall not stand in Thy sight: Thou hatest all workers of iniquity." What is it to stand in the sight of God? It is to be accepted of Him. We read in the first Psalm, "The ungodly shall not stand in the judgment." But will the ungodly not stand in the judgment; are not they the people that will have to stand before the great white throne? Yes: but they will have no standing there, because when He speaks of standing in the judgment, He means being acquitted, being accepted of God in that day. "The ungodly will not be acquitted in the judgment," and so here, "The foolish shall not be acquitted in Thy sight." In Revelation when the awful judgment of the last days will break over the world the cry goes forth, "The great day of His wrath is come; and who shall be able to stand?" (6:17). You see, your standing is to be accepted of God in that day.

Well, who will be able to stand? In the fifth chapter of Romans, verses 1 and 2, we read, "Therefore being justified by faith, we have peace with God through our Lord Jesus Christ: By whom also we have access by faith into this grace wherein we stand." Every believer has a standing before God of which the worldling knows nothing. The unsaved man has no standing, but every child of God stands complete in the risen Christ in all the infinite value of the precious atoning blood of Jesus.

Notice the second part of this verse, "Thou hatest all workers of iniquity." What does that mean? Are we wrong in telling men that no matter how sinful they are God loves them? We cannot be wrong for the Word itself says, "God so loved the world, that He gave His only begotten Son, that whosoever believeth in Him should not perish, but have everlasting life" (John 3:16), and that world is made up of sinners. What does, "Thou hatest all workers of iniquity" mean? God abhors the work of ungodly men. No matter how true it is that He loves the sinner, He hates his sin and longs to see the sinner separated from his sin. If men persist in continuing in their sin there can be nothing but banishment from God for eternity, and so destruction comes to the workers of iniquity. "Thou shalt destroy them that speak leasing: the Lord will abhor the bloody and deceitful man." And from this point on there seems to loom before the souls of the writers of these beautiful Old Testament hymns a strong and dreadful character who is the enemy of the people of God and the enemy of everything holy. In other words as you read, it seems that you can see the foreshadowing, all the way through, of the last great enemy of God's people, who is going to rise up just before the end, the antichrist, and he, I believe, is really "the bloody and deceitful man" that is in view here. We shall see other terms used of him as we go along.

In spite of all this the child of God can say today as the remnant of Israel will be able to say, "As for me, I will come into Thy house in the multitude of Thy mercy: and in Thy fear will I worship toward Thy holy temple. Lead me, O Lord, in Thy righteousness because of mine enemies; make Thy way straight before my face." In other words, all I want to know, Lord, is what Thy path is, and then I would have grace to walk in it. "There is no faithfulness in their mouth; their inward part is very wickedness; their throat is an open sepulchre." This passage is quoted in the third chapter of the Epistle to the Romans in describing the corruption of men out of Christ.

"They flatter with their tongue. Destroy Thou them, O God; let them fall by their own counsels; cast them out in the multitude of their transgressions; for they have rebelled against Thee." You say, Well that does not seem to be a very gracious kind of prayer. Why does David not rather pray that God will break them down and bring them to repentance and save their souls? You see, the Psalmist carries us on to a time of crisis when the enemies of God and the people of God on the other hand are engaged in the last great conflict, and the only way that righteousness can triumph in that time will be by the destruction of all the enemies of the Lord. People have often said that some of these Psalms, with their imprecations, seem so contrary to the spirit of Christ. Of course they have to do largely with law, and in the coming day of tribulation it will be law rather than grace that rules, but after all, do we not even now enter in measure to the same spirit?

About the close of the Civil War two gentlemen happened to meet in a railway train. One of them was sitting there reading his Bible when the other sat down by him and said, "My friend, I am rather surprised to see the Book you are reading; it is a Bible, is it not?"

"Yes," said the other, "it is."

"You look like an intelligent person; you don't mean to tell me you believe in the Bible?"

"Yes, I do believe in it."

"I didn't know any intelligent persons believed it any more. When I was young, I used to think it was all right, but when I got older I threw it overboard."

"What did you find in it so objectionable?"

"Well, take for instance those imprecatory Psalms. I cannot reconcile those with a loving God."

The other was going to answer him when a newsboy came hurrying through the car calling, "Extra! Extra! Grant is marching on Richmond!" and everybody wanted a paper. This man said, "Good! I am glad that Grant is getting down to business at last. I hope he will wipe Richmond off the face of the earth."

"My friend," said the other, "that is an imprecatory Psalm!"

What did that man mean? He did not really have any hatred in his heart toward the people of the south, but as he thought of the four long years of war he felt that the quickest way to end it all would be by the downfall of Richmond. And so, after all the long, long struggle between good and evil, when at last the end is just about reached and the army of Satan, marching under the antichrist, is defying God, the heart cries out to God to destroy these enemies and to let righteousness prevail. It does not imply hatred but an earnest desire that the long, long reign of wickedness should come to an end and the reign of righteousness begin.

On the other hand, "Let all those that put their trust in Thee rejoice: let them ever shout for joy, because Thou defendest them: let them also that love Thy name be joyful in Thee. For Thou, Lord, wilt bless the righteous; with favour wilt Thou compass him as with a shield." And so we think of the tried people of God today entering into these Psalms and finding in them suited vehicles for expression of the earnest desires of their hearts. But how much more will they have their application in that coming day when the remnant of Israel will be suffering so terribly under the hand of the beast and the antichrist. Wherever there is a measure of divine illumination the heart will be lifted above the trial and will be able to look up to God and count on Him while waiting for the hour when the King shall return to bring in the reign of righteousness.

THROUGH TRIAL TO GLORY
PSALMS 6 TO 8

IN THE SIXTH PSALM DAVID DEALS PARTICULARLY WITH the judgments of God and the need of mercy upon the part of the individual saint, for strange as it may seem, paradoxical as it may appear to say it, saints are sinners. What I mean by that is that though every believer in the Lord Jesus Christ has been sanctified in the sense that he is set apart to God in all the value of the finished work and the atoning blood of the Lord Jesus Christ, and therefore he is perfected forever in His sight, yet the fact remains that the believer himself is daily conscious of failure, and the closer he walks with God the more conscious he is of the sins of his own heart and life, and the more deeply penitent he is because of those shortcomings. It is quite possible, of course, to be so utterly out of fellowship with God that one can imagine he is living a sinless life, because he judges by the standards of the world without, and if he does not curse and swear and get drunk, he thinks he is living a holy life. But as one enters the presence of God and is overwhelmed with a sense of His infinite holiness he realizes there are things in his life so opposed to the holiness of God that it breaks him down in repentance before the Lord. Then the tendency is, not to feel that His dealings are too hard, but to wonder how God can be gracious at all, and it throws one on His mercy. That is the attitude of the Psalmist.

Notice the opening verses as he cries for mercy in that day of Jehovah's wrath, "O Lord, rebuke me not in Thine anger, neither chasten me in Thy hot displeasure. Have mercy upon me, O Lord; for I am weak: O Lord, heal me; for my bones are vexed. My soul is also sore vexed: but Thou, O Lord, how long?" In reading some of these Psalms we need to remember that Old Testament saints did not have the full, clear revelation of the grace of God that we have today, and therefore it was proper for David to cry, "O Lord, rebuke me not in Thine anger, neither chasten me in Thy hot displeasure." I do not need to pray that today. I know that "Whom the Lord loveth He chasteneth, and scourgeth every son whom He receiveth" (Heb. 12:6). I know that God's rebuke will never be in anger; His chastening will never be in hot displeasure. If He allows chastening to come upon me it is because His loving heart sees it is what I need to conform me more fully to the image of His Son. So I must learn to trust in the midst of trial, and glorify God in the fires.

In verses 4 to 7 we see the saint in the greatest distress, in such distress that he is hardly accountable for his own thoughts. He is perplexed, confused; he cannot understand God's dealings. His case is something like Job's. He knew that God was righteous; he knew that God was holy, and yet he knew that he had been attempting to walk with God, and so could not understand why the Lord seemed to be withdrawing Himself from him and giving him up to such deep and bitter grief and sorrow. It was the attempt to explain this that forms the problem of the book of Job. Listen to the Psalmist, "Return, O Lord, deliver my soul: oh save me for Thy mercies' sake." You can understand, for instance, God's dear remnant people suffering under the hand of the antichrist, driven away from the ordinary habitations of man, persecuted, cast out, starving to death perhaps or suffering terrible tortures, crying out, "O Lord, why is it I have to go through this? Look upon me in grace, save me for Thy mercies' sake," and then with death before him the soul cries, "For in death there is no remembrance of Thee: in Sheol [not the grave merely but that which is deeper than the grave, the abode of disembodied spirits, the unseen world] who shall give Thee thanks?" Do not take this as a doctrinal statement. It is not that. The materialists, the Christadelphians, the Russellites delight in a statement like that and say, "Don't you see, the Spirit of God has said, 'In death there is no remembrance of Thee: in Sheol who shall give Thee thanks?' Therefore, when people die they are unconscious until the day of their resurrection. 'The dead know not any thing' (Eccl. 9:5). That is what the Old Testament tells us." But he is speaking of the dead bodies. You go out to a cemetery and look around and say, "These dead, they know not anything," but that does not touch the question of the spirits of the dead. Here the Psalmist sees death ahead and sees one after another cut down by the enemy and says, "Lord, You cannot get any glory out of that. Would You not get more glory if they were living here on earth to praise You?" We know now with New Testament revelation what the Psalmist was not able to understand clearly. Our Lord Jesus has "brought life and immortality to light through the gospel" (2 Tim. 1:10); and now we know that for the believer to be absent from the body is to be present with the Lord, and we can say, "Yes, even in the unseen world we will give Him thanks; we will praise His name." When Paul was caught up into the third heaven he heard the praise of saints and "unspeakable words, which it is not lawful for a man to utter" (2 Cor. 12:4). But do not try to read back into the Old Testament, truth that it did not please God to reveal until New Testament times. It was when the Lord Jesus came into this scene that He took the cover, as it were, from the unseen world and revealed conditions beyond the grave.

The Psalmist continues, "I am weary with my groaning; all the night make I my bed to swim; I water my couch with my tears." Some of you think you have suffered a good deal. Have you ever wept so much that you soaked the bed clothes? David says that he did, when hunted out there by King Saul. You have not suffered as much as he; and think of what the coming remnant will have to go through. We are so inclined to self-pity. We do not remember that we "have not yet resisted unto blood, striving against sin" (Heb. 12:4). When I hear friends who have returned from Russia, and also during these days from China, tell of the terrible things that saints of God have had to pass through over there, the unspeakable tortures to which they have had to submit, I feel that I have never known anything of suffering, nor anything of trial. David knew much about suffering. The people of God in some of these lands I have spoken of and the people of God in the coming day will have to know much of suffering. We are living in comfort, and the little things that trouble us so much, a few years hence as we look back, will seem as nothing compared to the wonderful goodness of God. "Mine eye is consumed because of grief; it waxeth old because of all mine enemies."

But now in the closing verses of the Psalm you see the saint rising above these troubles; dreadful as they are he is able to rise above them because he fixes his eyes upon the Lord. When his eyes were upon the troubles they seemed insurmountable, but when he looks away from them to God, he strikes a note of confidence, "Depart from me, all ye workers of iniquity; for the Lord hath heard the voice of my weeping." Here we see faith in exercise. In the earlier part of the Psalm it was a poor, troubled heart, cast down and distressed because of unbelief; but now he has his eyes on God, and his troubles seem very small after all, and he cries, "Let all mine enemies be ashamed and sore vexed: let them return and be ashamed suddenly." It is a great thing when we have committed things to God, to say, not merely, "The Lord *will* undertake," but "The Lord *has* undertaken." I have put the thing in His hands, and I believe He has taken care of it. Take that beautiful word in another portion of Scripture, "Call upon Me in the day of trouble: I will deliver thee, and thou shalt glorify Me" (Psa. 50:15). I am in the day of trouble; I am distressed and say, "Dear me, I do not know what is going to happen. I am afraid everything I have counted on is going to pieces; I have no standing." When I talk this way, I act like a man who does not know the living God at all. He has said, "Call upon Me in the day of trouble: I will deliver thee, and thou shalt glorify Me" (Psa. 50:15). This is my day of trouble, and so I turn to Him and call upon Him, and then what? I go on with my head down just the same as ever. That is not faith. God has said, "Call upon Me." Lord, I called upon Thee; Thou hast promised and I dare to believe! That is what lifts me above the trial and enables me to triumph.

And so we pass on into the seventh Psalm and find that there is another thing we need to have before us when trouble comes. That is a clear conscience. The Apostle Paul said that he exercised himself "to have always a conscience void of offence toward God, and toward men" (Acts 24:16). If I have a bad conscience, if I have been living out of fellowship with God, if I have been doing things really wrong, when trouble comes and I want to go to God about it, I am not able to pray. David says, "If I regard iniquity in my heart, the Lord will not hear me" (Psa. 66:18). I try to go to Him and all the time these things come before me, and I cannot pray, so I need to be careful to keep short accounts with God, to be sure that I have a good conscience, and then I can go to Him in confidence.

In the seventh Psalm we have the Psalmist pleading for righteous judgment, and he says, "I am not conscious of deliberately and wilfully sinning against God." He knows he has failed, as all of us do, and as he expresses himself in the fifth Psalm; but there is such a thing as knowing that the main desire of your life has been for righteousness and that the main purpose of your life is to live for God. In the opening verses he expresses his trust, "O Lord my God, in Thee do I put my trust: save me from all them that persecute me, and deliver me: Lest he tear my soul like a lion, rending it in pieces, while there is none to deliver." And then he puts on the breastplate of righteousness. He is going to face the foe, and so looks into his own life and asks God to help him that he may look into it more carefully, and he says in verses 3 to 5: "O Lord my God, if I have done this; if there be iniquity in my hands; If I have rewarded evil unto him that was at peace with me; (yea, I have delivered him that without cause is mine enemy;) Let the enemy persecute my soul, and take if, yea, let him tread down my life upon the earth, and lay mine honour in the dust." His enemies were reproaching him with having done evil, and he says, "If I have done these things, I deserve to be ill-treated—let my enemy tread down my life upon the earth, and lay mine honour in the dust." But he knows as he looks into his own life that these things are not true. He has been seeking to glorify God, and so he can pray in confidence.

In verses 6 and 7 he calls on God to arise to his help: "Arise, O Lord, in Thine anger, lift up Thyself because of the rage of mine enemies: and awake for me to the judgment that Thou hast commanded"—I have put everything in Thine hand. I have put Thee between me and mine enemies, and I ask Thee to undertake, to do the things that should be done. I will trust Thee to do it "So shall the congregation of the people compass Thee about: for their sakes therefore return Thou on high." And then in perfect confidence he says, "The Lord shall judge the people: judge me, O Lord, according to my righteousness, and according to mine integrity that is in me." Do you say to me, "I would not like to say that to God; I would not like to say, 'Judge me according to my righteousness' because I really have no righteousness." No, man has none of his own, and David recognized that, but he is speaking now of what God by His grace hath wrought in him, and he is conscious of the fact that he has sought to walk before the Lord in integrity of heart. Somebody has well said, "The strings of David's harp were the chords of the heart of Jesus," and through all these Psalms you can hear the voice of our Lord Jesus. We sometimes point out certain Psalms, perhaps thirty or forty of them, and say they are Messianic Psalms because there is some definite reference in the New Testament that connects them with Christ, but there is a certain sense in which the suffering Saviour, committing Himself to the Father, may be traced right through the Psalms. In this world God often seems to treat His best friends worst, and He treated His own Son worst of all, and what does that tell us? All these hard and difficult things are working out for future blessing. Our Lord Jesus "endured the cross, despising the shame" because of the joy that was set before Him, and we as believers can say, "Our light affliction, which is but for a moment, worketh for us a far more exceeding and eternal weight of glory" (2 Cor. 4:17). But let us be sure that we walk with God in uprightness of spirit. If I try to pray and all the time my heart is accusing me of a lack of integrity, there is no liberty. If there has been evil in my life it must be judged.

Then in the next section of this Psalm, verses 9 and 10, notice how blessedly the Psalmist turns to God as his defense, "Oh let the wickedness of the wicked come to an end; but establish the just: for the righteous God trieth the hearts and reins"—that is the inward part. "My defence is of God, which saveth the upright in heart." And so no matter how the waters are rolling over him, he can count on God; he can believe that He will bring him through. Then in verses 11 to 17 he contemplates the divine government. God is still the moral Governor of the universe, and no matter what is going on it cannot get out of His hand. Only so much evil is permitted. "God judgeth the righteous, and God is angry with the wicked every day." And as Judge of the universe He is going to deal with wickedness. I do not have to do it. "If he turn not, He will whet His sword; He hath bent His bow, and made it ready. He hath also prepared for him the instruments of death; He ordaineth His arrows against the persecutors." God is going to turn around some day and is going to deal with those who are afflicting His saints. And so in verses 14 to 17 you get the end of the wicked, the judgment they shall yet have to endure. All the sorrows that God's people will ever have they know in this world. The moment they leave this scene behind there is nothing but endless blessing. On the other hand every bit of pleasure, every bit of joy, ever" bit of happiness of any kind that the worldling will ever know he gets down here; while for him there is nothing but sorrow beyond. You remember Abraham's words to that one-time rich man, "Son, remember that thou in thy lifetime receivedst thy good things, and likewise Lazarus evil things: but now he is comforted, and thou at tormented" (Luke 16:25).

A prize fighter who got converted had a little bit of a wife who was angry because he had become a Christian. In his unconverted days they went around to the theaters and all the worldly things, but now he would have none of it, and she would be perfectly furious and denounce his Christianity. One day she was going after him with a broom., and as he was trying to get out of her way he stumbled and fell, and she took advantage of that and pummelled him well. The door opened and an old friend of his stood there and watched the strange sight, and said, "Why, Bob, do you mean to say you would let a little woman like that pound you—you a former prize fighter!"

"Oh," he said, "she is getting all the heaven she will ever get in this world and as long as she is enjoying it I let her have it"

David emphasizes that in these last four verses: "Behold, he travaileth with iniquity, and hath conceived mischief, and brought forth falsehood. He made a pit, and digged it, and is fallen into the ditch which he made. His mischief shall return upon his own head, and his violent dealing shall come down upon his own pate. I will praise the Lord according to His righteousness: and will sing praise to the name of the Lord most high."

That brings us to the end of this period of suffering, for in the next Psalm we have the appearance of the Son of Man and see Him set over all things. It is a wonderful Psalm and it is referred to again and again in the New Testament. We are no longer occupied with vain man and his ungodly ways, not even with the sufferings of the people of God, but we turn away to consider the wonders of God's name and the glory of His creation. "O Lord our Lord, how excellent is Thy name in all the earth! who hast set Thy glory above the heavens. Out of the mouth of babes and sucklings hast Thou ordained strength because of Thine enemies, that Thou mightest still the enemy and the avenger."

The day has come when God arises to shake terribly the earth, to bring to an end the long ages of Satan's rule, to will the enemy and the avenger; and the Psalmist looks up and says: "When I consider Thy heavens, the work of Thy fingers, the moon and the stars, which Thou hast ordained; What is man, that Thou art mindful of him? and the son of man, that Thou visitest him?" Oh, says David, I feel so small. I thought I was so important before. My own grief and distresses so pressed upon me, but now when I look at the heavens and see those galaxies of suns with their surrounding planets in the heavens, universe after universe stretching out into infinity, I wonder that God pays any attention to me at all. "What is man, that Thou art [so] mindful of him? and the son of man, that Thou visitest him?" But God has His eyes on the Second Man, and it has pleased Him to appoint a time when man is to have absolute authority over this universe. God gave this authority to Adam, but Adam was not the son of Man and therefore this passage cannot be referring to him. It was God's purpose that man should hold this lower creation in subjection to himself, but he failed and so the Second Man comes into the scene, and He is before the eyes of God here, "Thou hast made Him a little lower than the angels, and hast crowned Him with glory and honour." It is our Lord Jesus Christ, as we know from Hebrews, who came from Godhead's glory and took a place lower than the angels. Do you realize that our Lord Jesus Christ is just as truly Man in glory as He was when here on earth? That is one of the most wonderful truths of Scripture for the comfort of our hearts. "There is … one Mediator between God and men, the *Man* Christ Jesus" (1 Tim. 2:5). Stephen said, "I see the heavens opened, and the Son of Man standing on the right hand of God" (Acts 7:56)—Jesus, a Man in glory crowned with glory and honor!

"Thou madest Him to have dominion over the works of Thy hands." Though Satan has sought so thwart God's purpose it is going to be carried out. "Thou hast put all things under His feet." In Hebrews we read, "Now we see not yet all things put under Him." We have only to walk the streets of Chicago to realize that all things are not yet put under His feet; but the writer goes on to say, "But we see Jesus, who was made a little lower than the angels for the suffering of death, crowned with glory and honour" (Heb. 2:8, 9). Therefore, knowing that God is going to carry out His purpose we do not see everything put under Him, but we do see Him put above everything, and not only in the moral world but in the lower creation as well.

"All sheep and oxen, yea, and the beasts of the field; The fowl of the air, and the fish of the sea, and whatsoever passeth through the paths of the seas." I love to think of the time when the groaning creation that has shared in the fall through no fault of its own, is going to be delivered from the bondage of corruption in the day of the manifestation of the glory of God. We learn from passages in Isaiah that blessing is to come to the very beasts of the field and the cattle. John Wesley prepared two or three sermons to show that cattle and beasts are going to heaven, for be thought that referred to heaven and that God was going to make up for all they suffered here by taking them to heaven at last. But Scripture speaks of them as "natural brute beasts, made to be taken and destroyed" (2 Pet. 2:12). What it does show is that when He reigns and everything is put under His feet, the lower creation will be delivered from the bondage of corruption and the very beasts will be brought into a more delightful existence than we have ever known.

And so he concludes this octave with the words, "O Lord our Lord, how excellent is Thy name in all the earth!" His heart is bubbling over with joy at the thought that God's Man, the Man of God's pleasure, the Son of Man whom He has made strong for Himself, is soon coming to be over all things. And so you can see what a complete picture we have of the ways of God, from the first advent of Christ to His second coming.

THE MAN OF THE EARTH
PSALMS 9 TO 12

WE COME NOW TO ANOTHER GROUP OF PSALMS THAT ARE all intimately linked together, and this time instead of an octave we have a septenary series. In the oldest Hebrew text there would be only six, for originally Psalms 9 and 10 were one. We do not know just when they were divided into two, but we know them as 9 and 10 instead of simply as 9. Then, if we add to them 11, 12, 13, 14, and 15, we have the series of seven.

In these first two Psalms, 9 and 10, we have the people of God in great distress and a sinister character oppressing and persecuting them. He is called, in the last verse of the 10th Psalm, "The man of the earth." That is very significant for our Lord Jesus is called, "The Second Man, the Lord from Heaven," and all through Scripture we can see hints in the Old Testament getting clearer and clearer as we move on into the New, of the man who in the last days comes out in vivid contrast to our Lord Jesus Christ. This man of the earth embodies in himself all earthly and carnal principles as our Lord Jesus embodies in Himself everything that is heavenly and spiritual. You remember when He was on earth He said to the Jews, "I am come in My Father's name, and ye receive Me not: if another shall come in his own name, him ye will receive" (John 5:43). He is undoubtedly referring to one who appears in many different parts of the Old Testament, the same one here called, "The man of the earth," the one who is spoken of in Daniel as "the king" who does "according to his will" (11:36); who is described in the prophet Zechariah as "the idol shepherd" (11:17) who left the flock and instead of tending and caring for them really persecuted them.

When you go farther on into the New Testament you get the name of this person, or perhaps it is more proper to say, his title. John says, "Ye have heard that antichrist shall come" and then he adds, "even now are there many antichrists; whereby we know that it is the last time" (1 John 2:18). But he shows that there will be a personal antichrist in the last days. The Apostle Paul speaks very definitely of him in the second chapter of the Second Epistle to the Thessalonians and calls him distinctly, The wicked one (2 Thess. 2:8). Our version calls him, That Wicked." It should be "That wicked one," or really, "The lawless one," and he is also called in that chapter, That man of sin" (Thess. 2:3). In the book of Revelation he is spoken of as "the false prophet" and as "another beast," the best that comes up out of the land, that is, the land of Palestine who "had two horns like a lamb and he spake as a dragon." The book of Revelation is the book of the Lamb, for you read of the Lamb twenty-nine times, but in the thirteenth chapter you have an imitation lamb, one who looks like a lamb but who speaks like a dragon; that is, he is energized by Satan. One of the oldest Christian fathers of the second century of the Christian era called him "Satan's firstborn." That is the imitation Christ. As we study these two Psalms I think we can see the shadow of this sinister personality falling across both these records, and we can get some idea of what it is going to mean for the remnant people of God in the land of Palestine after the Church of God has been caught away, in the time of Jacob's trouble, when the antichrist is reigning. His principle will be to rule or to ruin. If people will not own his authority, if they will not recognize him as their leader, then he will seek to destroy them. Therefore the people of God in that day will be suffering terribly under his hand.

We have had many forecasts of this personality. There have been, all down through the centuries both before the Christian era and since, persons who largely answered to the description of the antichrist. If one is familiar with the history of the people of Israel between the two Testaments he knows something of what the people of Israel suffered under the reign of Antiochus Epiphanes, he Syrian tyrant who has been called the Old Testament antichrist. Unless the Jews were ready to worship his false gods, to offer incense at his altars, he slaughtered them by the thousands and made the land run red with their blood. In the centuries since Christ was here on earth how many of these terrible tyrants there have been! No wonder that the early Christians thought first of Nero as the antichrist, later on of Domitian, and then afterwards when pagan Rome had fallen and papal Rome took its place, think of what Christians suffered under the papacy. Luther was firmly convinced that the papacy was the antichrist, that instead of one individual, that the man of sin was a system, the system of the papacy, seeking to destroy God's humble, loyal people who loved His Word and would not acknowledge papal substitutes. Then in later years under the awful tyranny in Russia, we are not surprised that poor, suffering Christians, hundreds of thousands of them martyred under the soviet government, have thought of Lenin and now of Stalin as the antichrist. In a certain sense all of these men were antichrists because, after all, the word just means, "opposed to Christ," and so wherever there is a tyrant who hates the gospel and hates the people of God and is opposed to Christ, he is in nature an antichrist. But all of these are just figures of the great antichrist yet to come. With that in view I think we can enter into the feelings of God's people in the coming day as we look carefully at these Psalms.

In Psalms 9 and 10 we have the man of the earth oppressing, destroying, ruthlessly seeking to root out of the world everything that is of God. In Psalms 11 to 15 we have the exercises of heart of God's people in view of all this. Of course we have those exercises in measure in Psalms 9 and 10, but these deal particularly with the tyrant of those days. Psalm 9 commences with a note of praise and, after all, no matter what God's people have to suffer, the marvelous thing is they have always been able to praise even when in the midst of the fire. That is one of the wonderful evidences of the divinity of Christianity. People can go through the most intense suffering, trial, and difficulty, and yet their hearts can be lifted above all the pain and anguish and grief and they can praise even in the fires. What a picture you have of that in Paul and Silas, cast into the inner prison, their backs bleeding, their feet made fast in the stocks, and instead of grumbling, instead of finding fault with God, instead of asking, "Why does God allow me, since I am His child, to suffer like this?" you find them singing praises to God and lifting their voices together in prayer until all the prisoners heard them. Then came the great earthquake and then the conversion of the jailer. Do you know anything else that can enable a man to glory in tribulation like that?

Listen to David, for David is the author of these Psalms, and he knew what it was to suffer. With Saul on the throne, he knew what it was to be driven out into the wilderness, persecuted, hated, forsaken, and yet to love in return. Instead of grumbling and complaining, his heart goes out in thanksgiving, "I will praise thee, O Lord, with my whole heart." Not with half a heart. And think of the people of God in that coming day in the midst of the greatest tribulation ever known, taking up these words on their lips, "I will praise Thee, O Lord, with my whole heart; I will shew forth all Thy marvelous works. I will be glad and rejoice in Thee." We may not be able to rejoice in circumstances, but we can always rejoice in Him, for God is above all circumstances. It is a bad thing when believers get under them. A brother said to another who he knew had not been well, "How are you, brother?"

"I am pretty well under the circumstances," he answered.

And the other said, "I am sorry to know that you are under the circumstances; I wish you could be above them. The Lord is able to lift you above them."

"Oh, yes," said the other, "I was not thinking of that."

We do not need to be under the circumstances. This man is above them all and he is rejoicing in spite of them. "I will sing praise to Thy name, O Thou most High." And then he tells you something of his confidence in God, for even when facing the enemy he can say, "When mine enemies are turned back, they shall fall and perish at Thy presence." You see, faith counts on God to keep His Word and knows that God has promised to give deliverance from the enemy, and so takes it for granted that this will occur. He says, "When mine enemies are turned back, they shall fall and perish at Thy presence. For Thou hast maintained my right and my cause; Thou satest in the throne judging right." No matter what conditions are like in the world around, the nations may rage, wars and rumors of war may cause the stoutest heart to tremble, but faith looks beyond it all and recognizes God as sitting on the throne, and knows that eventually He will bring out everything for His glory.

"Thou hast rebuked the heathen, Thou hast destroyed the wicked, Thou hast put out their name for ever and ever." It had not actually happened, but faith speaks of the things that are not as though they are. And then he turns and defies the enemy, "O thou enemy, destructions are come to a perpetual end." They are still carrying on the same bloody propaganda in Russia, but eventually God is going to arise for the deliverance of His people, and so here His saint cries out, "O thou enemy, destructions are come to a perpetual end: and thou hast destroyed cities; their memorial is perished with them."

In verses 7 to 12 the afflicted believer looks on and sees the Lord taking His great power and reigning in Zion. "But the Lord shall endure for ever: He hath prepared His throne for judgment. And He shall judge the world in righteousness, He shall minister judgment to the people in uprightness. The Lord also will be a refuge for the oppressed, a refuge in times of trouble. And they that know Thy name will put their trust in Thee: for Thou, Lord, hast not forsaken them that seek Thee." What about us at the present time? We do not know anything as yet of what many of the people of God have experienced in times of persecution and trial; we do not know anything of what the remnant of Israel will have to go through, and yet how often our heads hang down like bulrushes because things go a little hard with us, because we are up against misunderstanding, and we get so discouraged. Let us rather take a leaf out of the book of these saints of God who in the midst of awful persecution and trial could say, "They that know Thy name will put their trust in Thee: for Thou, Lord, has not forsaken them that seek Thee." God has never gone back on His Word, and He has never failed His people. But someone says, "He has left them to die; He has allowed them to be tortured and afflicted." Yes, that is true, but that was not defeat; for the very moment the soul left the body it was present with the Lord, and for all one ever suffered on earth He makes up abundantly yonder.

And so the Psalmist can exclaim, "Sing praises to the Lord, which dwelleth in Zion: declare among the people His doings." When reading the prophetic word (and the Psalms are as truly part of the prophetic word as the books that we think of in this connection, such as Isaiah, Jeremiah, etc.—the New Testament speaks of "the prophet David") we should remember that whenever it speaks of Zion and Mount Zion it means exactly what it says; it means Mount Zion. We have a way in Christendom of taking a lot of these terms that have to do with Israel and with their inheritance of the kingdom promised to them, over to Christianity and spiritualizing everything and so speak of the Church as being Mount Zion. When I was compiling a song book some years ago there was one song, which is used often in connection with missionary services, that I was very eager to have; it was that beautiful song, "O Zion Haste Thy Mission High Fulfilling." You know, Zion is not doing any missionary work at all, but I wanted that hymn, and so I changed the first line to, "O Christian haste thy mission high fulfilling." But some day Zion will have a mission of blessing to the whole world. That will be when the Lord Jesus reigns on Mount Zion, and He will reign there, for God is going to fulfill that word of the Psalmist David who by faith sees antichrist destroyed and sees the Lord dwelling in Zion. "Declare among the people His doings."

And then He remembers that God is never going to forget anything that His people have suffered. Have you had to suffer, and have you felt utterly forsaken and forgotten? God never forgets. You may say, "But others have treated me so badly." He knows all about that. Look at verse 12, "When He maketh inquisition for blood, He remembereth them: He forgetteth not the cry of the humble." He takes note of every sorrow that His people have to go through, and in the day of judgment there will be stern retribution for those who have caused suffering to His people.

Then from verse 13 to the end of verse 17 you have another distinct section in which the Psalmist tells some of his personal experiences. "Have mercy upon me, O Lord; consider my trouble which I suffer of them that hate me, Thou that liftest me up from the gates of death: That I may shew forth all Thy praise in the gates of the daughter of Zion: I will rejoice in Thy salvation. The heathen are sunk down in the pit that they made: in the net which they hid is their own foot taken." Is that not true today? How utterly helpless they are. They do not know how to get out of the pit into which they have sunk, but it will be a thousand times worse in this day of which we read, "The Lord is known by the judgment which He executeth: the wicked is snared in the work of his own hands."

And then notice those two queer looking words at the end of verse 16, "Higgaion. Selah." You do not need to read them, for they are not part of the Psalm. They are simply instructions to the choir leader. "Higgaion" is a type of Hebrew music to which this Psalm was to be sung, and "Selah" is like one of those little rest marks that we have, to give the choir a chance to breathe before they go on. It comes in such a solemn way here for he is going to say a very serious thing in the next verse; but first he says, just rest a moment; pause a moment. He tells us something the world does not like to hear, something that men do not want to believe, but here it is in God's Holy Word: "The wicked shall be turned into hell, and all the nations that forget God." There is something about that, that has a very strange effect on the child of God, for while his heart goes out in sympathy as he thinks of the awful doom toward which the wicked are sinking, yet it enables him to lift his heart in praise as he thinks of the judgment from which he has been saved. When I think of what hell means, it ought to fill my heart with great compassion as I look upon the multitudes about me. On the other hand, how I should praise the One who has redeemed me from such a doom!

Years ago when I was a Salvation Army officer we used to sing a song the chorus of which is:

> *"Let the white glare of Thy throne be cast*
> *O'er each step of the way that I go,*
> *And the red, red light from the lake of the lost*
> *O'er each hour shed its lurid, awful glow."*

Often when speaking to God in prayer those words come to me, and I say to God, "I do want to live day by day in view of the great white throne and in view of the lake of fire toward which men and women are hastening in their sins so that I shall not be indifferent to the needs of souls around." I do not understand how a child of God could ever harbor malice or ill feeling even toward those who are causing him suffering when he thinks of the doom toward which they are hastening. When the Psalmist thinks of the judgment to which the godless nations are going, his heart is stirred to compassion as he thinks of the grace that delivered him from it all, and his voice is lifted in praise. In the last three verses he thanks God for His mercies, and yet calls on Him to bring the sufferings of His people to an end.

"For the needy shall not always be forgotten: the expectation of the poor shall not perish for ever." This is the time when it looks as though the needy are forgotten, but it will not always be so. "Arise, O Lord; let not man prevail: let the heathen be judged in Thy sight. Put them in fear, O Lord: that the nations may know themselves to be but men." There is another rest, and then he goes right on into the tenth Psalm.

In the two opening verses he has the lawless one before him and cries to God as his refuge, "Why standest Thou afar off, O Lord? why hidest Thou Thyself in times of trouble?" This will be the time of Jacob's trouble. We never would have people asking the question, "Will the Church go through the great tribulation?" if they could understand that the great tribulation is not the time of the Church's trouble, but that it is the time of Jacob's trouble, and the judgments of the tribulation are not to be poured out on the Church but on those that dwell on the earth. The Church is to be taken out of the scene before that time begins. Here you have in view the people, the remnant of Israel, the seed of Jacob, but this is the last trouble they will have to go through before the Lord brings them into the blessings of the kingdom. Here you see this wicked one who seeks to destroy the people of God in that day, "The wicked [really, the wicked one, the lawless one, the same one that Paul refers to in 2 Thessalonians 2] in his pride doth persecute the poor." And there are others associated with him. "Let them be taken in the devices that they have imagined. For the wicked boasteth of his heart's desire, and blesseth the covetous, whom the Lord abhorreth."

From verses 4 to 11 you have a description of the wicked one, the evil character of this lawless one. It is really the antichrist himself that comes before us. "The wicked, through the pride of his countenance, will not seek after God: God is not in all his thoughts. His ways are always grievous; Thy judgments are far above out of his sight: as for all his enemies, he puffeth at them." He imagines that he is going to subject everything to himself. He knows very little of what God is doing or has planned. "He hath said in his heart, I shall not be moved: for I shall never be in adversity." How often tyrants of this world have taken that haughty position. We read that, when Mussolini was shot at and might have been killed, he laughed it off and said, The bullet has never been made that can kill me." He felt he was absolutely superior to all the efforts of his foes to destroy him. And so the antichrist says in his heart, "I shall not be moved: for I shall never be in adversity."

"His mouth is full of cursing and deceit and fraud: under his tongue is mischief and vanity. He sitteth in the lurking places of the villages: in the secret places doth he murder the innocent: his eyes are privily set against the poor." Not he personally, of course, but through his agents. You can see this taking place in Russia: the secret police on the lookout for any who serve the Lord in order to entrap them. "He lieth in wait secretly as a lion in his den: he lieth in wait to catch the poor: he doth catch the poor, when he draweth him into his net. He croucheth, and humbleth himself, that the poor may fall by his strong ones. He hath said in his heart, God hath forgotten: He hideth His face; He will never see it." He thinks that God has nothing to do with these things and that he can have things his own way.

Now in the closing verses of this Psalm David again, as representing the remnant suffering under the hand of antichrist, lifts up the heart in prayer to God for deliverance, "Arise, O Lord; O God, lift up Thine hand: forget not the humble. Wherefore doth the wicked contemn God? he hath said in his heart, Thou wilt not require it Thou hast seen it" This man of the earth, this lawless one may think that God is indifferent; he may think that there is no God; he may be atheistic in his belief, but God has seen and God knows. "Thou hast seen it; for Thou beholdest mischief and spite, to requite it with Thy hand: the poor committeth himself unto Thee." Is not that a lovely verse? If you are in distress, will you not take it for yourself? "The poor committeth himself unto Thee." That is better than committing yourself to the civic authorities. He will undertake. "Thou art the helper of the fatherless." How often God has pledged Himself to be a Father to the fatherless.

"Break Thou the arm of the wicked and the evil man: seek out his wickedness till Thou find none." In other words, seek him out until he is destroyed and cannot do any more evil. Is that not a vindictive thing to pray? In those dark days when Japan overran China did you not feel like praying, "Lord, destroy the Japanese army so that it cannot do any more wickedness in China"? Think of the thousands of women, children, and babies who were destroyed. Would it not be right for Christians to pray, "Lord, put a stop to all that"? Surely it would. We have a kind of pacifist idea nowadays that we must just look on and not be upset by anything. But that is not the spirit of the Bible. We have a right to call on God to put a stop to wickedness. Then he says, "The Lord is King for ever and ever: the heathen [nations] are perished out of His land." It is as though he sees all those nations gathered together in Palestine, as they will be, and sees the judgment of God executed and the nations perished out of His land, and His land is Emmanuel's land.

"Lord, Thou hast heard the desire of the humble: Thou wilt prepare their heart, Thou wilt cause Thine ear to hear: To judge the fatherless and the oppressed, that the man of the earth may no more oppress." And the man of the earth is the antichrist.

And now in the last five Psalms of this series you have what might be likened to a little song book, a hymn book for the oppressed people of God in that dark day. Do you know why the people of Scotland love the Psalms so much? They learned to love them when they were being persecuted by those who sought to destroy the Scottish church; and when the Covenanters had to hide in the hills for their safety they sang these Psalms as fitting their exact circumstances, and how much they meant to them. There they were, driven out on the mountainside to hold their meetings for worship and for prayer and praise. It must have been a wonderful thing to hear a company of them lifting up their voices in one of these Psalms.

Suppose you were one of the remnant of Israel in the coming day and you have met with a few of His people while the agents of the antichrist are spying on you. How beautifully these Psalms would fit as you would lift up the heart to God. "In the Lord put I my trust: how say ye to my soul, Flee as a bird to your mountain?" Is it not strange that people would ever sing that old song, "Flee as a bird to your mountain"? It suggests that it is perfectly right to flee as a bird to your mountain, but that is not what David is telling us here. He says, "My trust is in the Lord—though the people may say, 'Flee as a bird to your mountain,' I will not do it; I will go to the Lord Himself for He is my refuge; He is my strength. I need to go to Him"—"for, lo, the wicked bend their bow, they make ready their arrow upon the string, that they may privily shoot at the upright in heart. If the foundations be destroyed, what can the righteous do? The Lord is in His holy temple, the Lord's throne is in heaven: His eyes behold, His eyelids try, the children of men. The Lord trieth the righteous: but the wicked and him that loveth violence His soul hateth." The wicked are looking on; they know that the day is near when the Lord will be manifested and, "Upon the wicked He shall rain snares, fire and brimstone, and an horrible tempest: this shall be the portion of their cup. For the righteous Lord loveth righteousness; His countenance doth behold the upright."

All of these Psalms, up to Psalm 15, express the same thing, the suffering people, the afflicted people committing their cause to God and counting on Him to bring them through in triumph at last.

THE CRY OF GOD'S PEOPLE
PSALMS 13 TO 15

IN PSALM 13 WE HAVE THE TRIED BELIEVER CRYING TO God for deliverance and yet trusting in His overruling providence in spite of all the difficult circumstances of the way. Four times in the first two verses we get the cry, "How long?" "How long wilt thou forget me, O Lord? for ever? how long wilt thou hide Thy face from me? How long shall I take counsel in my soul, having sorrow in my heart daily? how long shall mine enemy be exalted over me?" This is the heart cry, not only of Christian people during this present age of grace when we have to suffer for righteousness' sake, but also it is the cry of God's earthly people, Israel, who, ever since that dread hour when they exclaimed, "His blood be on us, and on our children" (Matt. 27:25), have been suffering terribly because they failed to recognize their King when He came to bring deliverance.

While on our trip to the Holy Land my wife and my daughter and I stood by the Wailing Wall of Jerusalem, and for something like an hour we watched the Jews, several hundreds of them, as they faced that wall, all that is left of the great structure that Solomon once built (the Mohammedans have control of the temple area above), and we heard them repeating these cries from the Psalms. Mournfully these words rang out, "How long? How long shall the enemy oppress? How long shall Thy people suffer? How long till Messiah comes and brings deliverance?" As we stood with them we too cried, "How long?" and we prayed with them, "Even so, come, Lord Jesus," for we knew what they do not yet know, that deliverance will come with the return of our blessed Lord. And so the righteous here are crying to God for this deliverance.

"Consider and hear me," they pray, "O Lord my God: lighten mine eyes, lest I sleep the sleep of death." It is a very striking fact that death is presented both in the Old and New Testaments for the people of God as a sleep. That does not mean that when we put the bodies of our loved ones in Christ, away in the tomb, we bury all there is of them, that spirit, soul, and body go to sleep until the resurrection; for we know from Scripture that for the believer to be absent from the body is to be present with the Lord. When Christians die, they go directly to be with Christ, but the body sleeps, and that is what the Psalmist has in mind here. "Lighten mine eyes, lest I sleep the sleep of death; Lest mine enemy say, I have prevailed against him; and those that trouble me rejoice when I am moved." In spite of difficult circumstances the saint of God looks up in confidence and says, "But I have trusted in Thy mercy; my heart shall rejoice in Thy salvation. I will sing unto the Lord, because He hath dealt bountifully with me." I do not know anything but the salvation of God that can enable people to joy in the midst of sorrow and to praise in the hour of trial. The world has its Stoics, men who look at things in a philosophical kind of way and say, "I am not going to complain nor show the white feather," and so they grit their teeth and go on. That is a great thing. A lot of folk have not attained even to that. But that is not Christianity. Christianity enables one not only to endure uncomplainingly, but it also fills the heart and lips with songs in the night of sorrow and enables one to glory in tribulation. And so will it be with God's people in the dark, dark days when the antichrist will be manifested and they will be suffering under his cruel and wicked rule.

In the fourteenth Psalm we have a picture of the whole world since Christ's rejection. "The fool hath said in his heart, There is no God." Perhaps he does not say it with his lips; perhaps he would not call himself an atheist, but he acts as though there is no God. Any man is a fool who lives in a world like this as though there is no God. As you look at the Psalm you will see that the words, "there is" are in italics, which means that there is nothing in the original to answer to them. They are added to make the sentence a little clearer. Let us leave them out: "The fool hath said in his heart, No God"—no God for me, no God in my life, no God in my thinking—I am going to have my own way; I am going to do as I please; I am going to have my fling; I am going to live as I want to live! "Fools make a mock at sin" (Prov. 14:9). I know the world looks on the Christian and says, "Those are the fools—those people who have given up the joys of this world; who have turned away from the good times earth has to offer." Well, says the Apostle Paul, call us that if you like, "We are fools for Christ's sake" (1 Cor. 4:10), and after all "The foolishness of God is wiser than men" (1 Cor. 1:25). The real fool is the man who has no place for God in his life.

"They are corrupt, they have done abominable works, there is none that doeth good." These are the words quoted in the third chapter of the Epistle to the Romans where Paul brings the whole world, as it were, into court and lines them up and says, as it were, "Let me see, how do you stand? Guilty or not guilty?" He finds them all guilty of sinning against God, and he gives the verdict, "None that doeth good."—"There is none that understandeth, there is none that seeketh after God" (Rom. 3:12, 11), and he quotes from this Psalm to sustain that judgment. "The Lord looked down from heaven upon the children of men," and He says, "There is none that understandeth, there is none that seeketh after God." Is there any man anywhere, anybody who, following the bent of his natural mind, understands the purpose of his creation and really desires to seek after God? No; He says, there are none. "They are all gone aside, they are all together become filthy." What a filthy thing sin is! "There is none that doeth good, no, not one."

And then he charges the workers of iniquity with acting as men who are absolutely destitute of common sense: "Have all the workers of iniquity no knowledge?" Is it because they are utterly stupid that they live as they do? Sin is a terribly stupid thing, for a man knows, if he stops to think, that he cannot escape the consequences of sin. "Be not deceived; God is not mocked; for whatsoever a man soweth, that shall he also reap" (Gal. 6:7). What a stupid thing it is to go on sinning against God. No man in his right mind could ever do the things that some ungodly people do. "Who eat up My people as they eat bread, and call not upon the Lord." You would think that common sense would hold people back from some of the crimes and iniquities they are guilty of, but when sin gets a hold on a man it perverts his judgment

"There were they in great fear: for God is in the generation of the righteous," and He notes all that ungodly men are doing. He notices all the suffering and scorn that they heap upon His people. "When He maketh inquisition for blood, He remembereth them" (Psa. 9:12). Some day He will take matters into His own hands; meantime ungodly men shame "the counsel of the poor, because the Lord is his refuge." And then the Psalmist cries, as he yearns; for the coming of the Lord Jesus, Israel's Messiah, to put everything right: "Oh that the salvation of Israel were come out of Zion! when the Lord bringeth back the captivity of His people, Jacob shall rejoice, and Israel shall be glad." We see Israel going back to the land of Palestine now, but they are going back in unbelief. It is true that it is in fulfillment of prophecy which shows many of them are to be back in their own land before Christ comes, and so they are going back rejecting the Saviour. But some day He will appear, and when He does, the salvation of Israel will come out of Zion. When He came the first time, the Saviour came out of Bethlehem, but in that future day the Word of God, the message of God, is going forth from Mount Zion when God's King has been set upon His holy hill. And in that day when Christ reigns, who are the men who will have access into His presence, who are the people on whom He will look with complacency? These proud, haughty, careless worldlings who now seem to have things their own way? No; the Lord Jesus has said, "Blessed are the meek: for they shall inherit the earth" (Matt. 5:5). Oh, you say, those are the very people who need not expect to inherit much of this earth! If you do not stand up for your own rights and fight for them you do not get very far in this world. But Jesus says, "I am meek and lowly in heart" (Matt. 11:29), and He is going to rule from the river to the ends of the earth, and those that manifest His spirit and have become partakers of the divine nature are the ones who will reign with Him in that day.

And so, in the fifteenth Psalm the Psalmist says, "Lord, who shall abide in Thy tabernacle? who shall dwell in Thy holy hill?" And now note the answer, "He that walketh uprightly, and worketh righteousness, and speaketh the truth in his heart" Oh, you say, I thought people were saved by grace. I did not know folk were saved by works. I thought the Word of God distinctly tells us that it is "Not by works of righteousness which we have done, but according to His mercy He saved us, by the washing of regeneration, and renewing of the Holy Ghost" (Tit 3:5). Well, you thought right, but he is not speaking of salvation here; he is speaking of more than salvation, of reward in that coming day. He is speaking of those who shall reign with Christ, and who are they? Those who by newness of life prove the reality of the regeneration which they profess. They say they have been born of God; they say they have been justified by faith; they say that not by works of their own but by the finished work of Christ they have been converted; they have been made the righteousness of God in Christ, but how will other people know that? Simply because we tell them? They may question what we say; they must see a changed life, and those who in that coming day will find their place with Christ are those who manifest the new nature. He is not speaking of salvation here but of its manifestation. Do not talk about being made the righteousness of God in Christ if you do not work righteousness. If you are justified by faith, then you have received a new and righteous nature and your life should be a righteous life. He that "worketh righteousness, and speaketh the truth in his heart." God says He desires "truth in the inward parts" (Psa. 51:6).

"Who shall abide in Thy tabernacle? who shall dwell in Thy holy hill?" "He that backbiteth not with his tongue." What is it to backbite with your tongue? To speak people fair to the face and to say unkind things about people behind their backs. Do you know anybody that does that? If you have a looking glass at home, take a good look in it and see whether you can see any one in that glass that ever backbites with his tongue, and if you do, get down on your knees and tell the Lord that you are ashamed of yourself and that by His grace you will seek to have a kind word for others instead of saying something unkind. You will be surprised to see how much happier you will be and how many more friends you will make. It is all right to talk about people behind their back if you say the right thing. Let us be among those who never backbite with the tongue.

"Nor doeth evil to his neighbour, nor taketh up a reproach against his neighbour." He neither does that which definitely harms his neighbor, nor does he pick up a story from someone else and spread it abroad. He is seeking to help instead of to hinder. "In whose eyes a vile person is contemned; but he honoureth them that fear the Lord." Instead of standing with and endorsing the tactics of the vile person, he judges all that. In Proverbs 25:23 we read, "The north wind driveth away rain: so doth an angry countenance a backbiting tongue." Somebody comes to you and says, "Did you hear about Brother So and So?"

"No!" you say.

"Oh, it is something dreadful."

You say, "I do not wish to hear it!" and look as fierce as you can and you will drive him away. Stop that scandal instead of saying, "Oh, tell me about it!" and then going to the phone and spreading it. That is the way fellowship is broken. But if you will meet the backbiter with an angry countenance, instead of breaking fellowship you will maintain it.

And then notice: "He that sweareth to his own hurt, and changeth not." That is, if he settles it with God that he is going to do a certain thing, even though he finds out afterward that it does not seem to be to his benefit, he says, I am going on and do it anyway. If he has said, "Lord, I am going to give so and so to Thy work," and then things get hard, and he thinks, "I guess I cannot give the Lord what I intended; I need that money for things for myself," and so he spends the money on himself and has no more to spare. But if he says, "But I have opened my mouth to the Lord and cannot go back," and he deals faithfully with God, he finds that they that honor God are honored of Him.

"He that putteth not out his money to usury." It is perfectly right and proper in a business way to invest money and get interest for it. The parable of the talents makes that clear, "Thou oughtest therefore to have put my money to the exchangers, and then at my coming I should have received mine own with usury" (Matt. 25:27). But if a brother or a sister is in need and you have the money to help and they come to you and you say, "Well, yes, I am willing to help. What security can you give?"

"I am sorry but I have none except the word of a Christian man or woman."

"Well, how much interest will you pay?" That is asking usury.

That is the thing that God's Word condemns. His people of old were not allowed to take interest from money loaned to their brethren, and the "Righteousness of the law [is] fulfilled in us, who walk not after the flesh, but after the Spirit" (Rom. 8:4). These are some very practical things, and a lot of us would get a great deal more blessing if we lived them out.

"Nor taketh reward against the innocent," that is, would not profit through the stumbling of another. "He that doeth these things shall never be moved." In other words, this Psalm sets before us the things that should characterize the child of God as he is passing through this world waiting for the coming of the righteous King, and when the King comes, he will stand before Him with perfect confidence to receive His approbation and to reign with Him in that day.

THE MAN CHRIST JESUS
PSALM 16

IT IS IN THE LAST CHAPTER OF THE GOSPEL OF LUKE THAT we read of our blessed Lord overtaking those two disciples on the way from Jerusalem to Emmaus, and He entered into their conversation as they were speaking together of Him, without at first giving them to know who it was that was walking with them. They were sad and He inquired the cause of it, and they told about Jesus and their hopes and how those hopes had been shattered by His crucifixion; but then they also added that certain women of the company who had been to the sepulcher that morning declared that they had seen a vision of angels who said that Jesus was now alive, but it was very evident they did not believe this; and then we read in verse 25, "He said unto them, O fools." The word there does not have quite the obnoxious meaning that our word "fool" has. It really means "simple ones." "O simple ones, and slow of heart to believe all that the prophets have spoken: Ought not Christ to have suffered these things, and to enter into His glory? And beginning at Moses and all the prophets, He expounded unto them in all the scriptures the things concerning Himself." I never read that but I think what a wonderful privilege those disciples had that day, and what a marvelous thing it would have been if that Bible reading of the Lord Jesus Christ had been delivered to a large audience with a stenographer sitting to one side so that we today could read that wonderful opening up of all the Scriptures that have to do with the things concerning Him. Why did He not give us such a book as that? It would have made a wonderful volume. Is not the reason this: He would have each one of us study the Word for ourselves in dependence on the Holy Spirit. He has just given us enough here to let us know that He is the theme of all Scripture, that wherever you turn in the Word of God, the subject is Jesus. And one thing I am sure of—on that day as they walked along, among the many portions of the Word that He expounded to them, was this sixteenth Psalm.

I suppose you have noticed the place this Psalm had in the ministry of the apostles afterward, in the book of Acts. In the second chapter of Acts, where we have Peter's great sermon on the day of Pentecost, you find him quoting from it and applying it to our Lord Jesus Christ (ver. 25). "David speaketh concerning Him, I foresaw the Lord always before my face, for He is on my right hand, that I should not be moved: Therefore did my heart rejoice, and my tongue was glad; moreover also my flesh shall rest in hope: Because Thou wilt not leave my soul in hell, neither wilt Thou suffer Thine Holy One to see corruption. Thou hast made known to me the way of life; Thou shalt make me full of joy with Thy countenance." And then listen to Peter's comment on it: "Men and brethren, let me freely speak unto you of the patriarch David, that he is both dead and buried." Why does he speak of David? David wrote this Psalm, but he pointed out that David was not writing of himself. Verse 30, "Therefore being a prophet" Many do not realize that David was a prophet, but the Psalms are all prophetic, and that in a most marvelous way. "Therefore being a prophet, and knowing that God had sworn with an oath to him, that of the fruit of his loins, according to the flesh, He would raise up Christ to sit on His throne; He seeing this before spake of the resurrection of Christ, that His soul was not left in hell, neither His flesh did see corruption. This Jesus hath God raised up, whereof we all are witnesses."

And then if you turn over to the thirteenth chapter of the book of Acts you will see how the Apostle Paul refers to the second Psalm in verse 32: "And we declare unto you glad tidings, how that the promise which was made unto the fathers, God hath fulfilled the same unto us their children, in that He hath raised up Jesus again; as it is also written in the second psalm, Thou art My Son, this day have I begotten Thee." Now that Psalm we have already looked at, and we have seen its application to Christ. Notice how this links up with what follows: "And as concerning that He raised Him up from the dead, now no more to return to corruption, He said on this wise, I will give you the sure mercies of David. Wherefore He saith also in another psalm, Thou shalt not suffer Thine Holy One to see corruption." He is referring to the sixteenth Psalm. "For David, after he had served his own generation by the will of God, fell on sleep, and was laid unto his fathers, and saw corruption. But He, whom God raised again, saw no corruption." So we may be quite sure that our Lord Jesus opened up this Psalm to His disciples that day. And later on during the forty days that He was with them after His resurrection and before His ascension, expounding unto them the things of the kingdom of God, we can be certain He went through all these Old Testament scenes and gave them an explanation of these Scriptures such as they had never had before, and this accounts for the fact that from the day of Pentecost on, these disciples seemed so quick in applying them. They quoted again and again from the Old Testament, and to no book did they delight to refer so much as to the book of Psalms.

Now in the first seven chapters of the book of Leviticus we have five distinct offerings, which present in various ways the perfection of the Person and the work of our Lord Jesus Christ, and it is an interesting fact that there are five Psalms which link in a special way with those five offerings. For instance, the first offering is the burnt offering. When you turn over to the fortieth Psalm, you find that is the Psalm of the burnt offering. Then for the moment passing over the second offering, the third is the peace offering; and if you turn over to the eighty-fifth Psalm you have the Psalm of the peace offering. That is followed by the sin offering, and Psalm twenty-two is the Psalm of the sin offering. And then that of the trespass offering. Psalm sixty-nine is the Psalm of the trespass offering.

I have passed over the meal offering or food offering. According to the old English way of speaking, the word "meat" took in all the repast. Our forbears would say, "They sat down to meat." It did not mean simply flesh. The meal offering did not have any flesh in it. The burnt, the peace, the sin, and the trespass offerings—in all these, animals were sacrificed, but not in the case of the meal offering. It was an offering made of fine flour mingled with oil, and it spoke not of the work of our Lord Jesus Christ, but of the perfection of His glorious Person, and it was the food of the priests of God. With all the other offerings the people were to bring the meal offering, and all these meal offerings were cakes or loaves made of fine flour. You housewives know the feeling of fine flour, not a coarse grain in it, and that typified the perfect Humanity of the Lord Jesus. So it spoke of the Lord Jesus' perfect Humanity. I think if the Lord wanted to make a meal offering typical of me, he would have to make it of old-fashioned, Scotch, steel-cut meal, because there are so many sharp edges to me, and that would picture me perfectly. But when it was the Lord Jesus Christ, there was no roughness, no sharp edges, no eccentricities; everything was perfect in His wonderful character. The meal offering was made of fine flour mingled with oil, and oil is a type of the Holy Spirit of God, and you remember that Christ was born of the Spirit. The angel told His mother Mary that the power of the Highest would overshadow her and she would bring forth a Son, and from the moment Christ came into the world you have the mingling of the oil and the fine flour. This offering, as I said, was the food of the priests. And what is our food as believers? We are to feed upon Christ in the presence of God. You say, "Well, I do not understand it." We feed on Christ by meditating on Christ. Where do we get Christ? Right in His Word and therefore we feed on Christ as we read His Word and meditate on the precious things which are revealed concerning His perfections and His matchless glory. Now this sixteenth Psalm may appropriately be called the Psalm of the meal offering. For this is the Psalm that brings before us the perfection of the Humanity of our Lord Jesus Christ. Have you ever stopped to consider this: the Lord Jesus, though He was God over all, chose in grace to become a dependent man down here in this world? You say, What do you mean by a *dependent* man? Well, I mean that He chose to come down here and set aside His own will and just be dependent on the will of God. In other words, He came here to live a life of faith. He is called "the author and finisher of … faith." There is a little word in the Epistle to the Hebrews, "finisher of *our* faith." But that is not what the Apostle said. He said He is the "author and finisher of faith." He chose to be a man of faith. That comes out in the scene in the wilderness when Satan came to Him, when He had a true human body, and it was sustained by food as ours. After those forty days he must have been very hungry indeed, and Satan said, "If Thou be the Son of God, command that these stones be made bread" (Matt. 4:3). Could He have made bread out of stones? Oh, yes; but He had no word from the Father to do it, and He had chosen to be dependent on the Father in everything. He was not going to make bread out of stones in obedience to a suggestion from the devil. So He said, "Man shall not live by bread alone, but by every word that proceedeth out of the mouth of God" (Matt. 4:4). He was a lowly Man of faith in this scene, living on the Word of God that proceeded out of the mouth of God.

In the sixteenth Psalm we hear Him speak to His Father. What did He have to pray about? Well, we know what He said on one occasion. In the seventeenth of John we hear Him praying for His own. Many of these Psalms were the prayers of Jesus. It has been said, "The strings of David's harps are the chords of the heart of Jesus." And as you read these Psalms you are listening to the breathings of the heart of Jesus. Listen to Him: "Preserve me, O God: for in Thee do I put my trust." Now in the Epistle to the Hebrews that is applied to Him. He is the Man of faith here on earth. He went through this scene for thirty-three years in perfect subjection to the Father's will—never attempting a step, never professing to give a revelation until He heard the Father's voice, and He chose as Man on earth to learn from His own Bible what the mind of God was. They were surprised when on one occasion the Lord said, speaking of His second coming, "Of that day and that hour knoweth no man, no, not the angels which are in heaven, neither the Son, but the Father" (Mark 13:32). What did He mean? Did He not know all things? Yes, as God, but He chose to lay aside the use of His own omniscience; He chose not to draw on His infinite knowledge, but to learn from the Scriptures and to get the word from the Father from day to day; and because there was nothing in the Scripture that told when His second coming would take place, He could say: "Of that day … knoweth no man." That helps us to see how truly He became Man, and how truly He lived a life of dependence on God.

The second verse is very striking. "O My soul, Thou hast said." Now you must notice the different words for "Lord." Wherever it is in small caps as here in the first instances, it translates the word "Jehovah." When it is lower case, it is the Lord and Master. Read it like this: "O My soul, Thou hast said unto Jehovah, Thou art My Master." Who is speaking? The Lord Jesus Christ, and He is addressing His own soul. He says, "O, My soul Thou hast said unto the LORD, Thou art My Master." In other words, "I am Thy servant." He came to the earth to be the Servant of Jehovah, the Servant of the Godhead. "My goodness extendeth not to Thee; But to the saints that are in the earth, and to the excellent, in whom is all My delight." What does He mean by that? Well, as God the Father looked down on the Lord Jesus, as He walked through this world, what did He see in Him? Absolute perfection. He was perfect in goodness; He was righteous in everything, in thought and word and deed. Scripture says "He knew no sin," "He did no sin," "in Him is no sin"; and yet He looks up to the Father and says, "My goodness extendeth not to Thee; But to the saints that are in the earth and to the excellent, in whom is all My delight." What then did He mean by that? Is it not this: "My Father, I am not pleading My goodness for Myself before Thee, but I am here on earth to do Thy will and to walk the path of righteousness on behalf of others. My goodness extendeth to the saints, the excellent in the earth, in whom is all My delight." Who were these saints, who were the excellent in the earth? Well, strange as it seems to say it, they were people who knew they were sinners and confessed it. When John the Baptist came preaching in the wilderness "Repent ye," he called on the people who owned their sin and guilt to be baptized with the baptism of repentance for the remission of sin. What did it mean? It meant this: the King is coming, and you have been waiting for Him, but you are not ready for Him. A lot of you are living in sin; many of you are selfish and proud; many of you are hypocritical. Get right with God; face your sin. If you own yourself a sinner, come down to the Jordan and let me baptize you. Poor sinners came to John and said, "John, you are right. God is righteous and we are unrighteous; you baptize us as confessed sinners." As John put them down beneath the waters of Jordan, it was just another way of saying, "These people deserve to die and they are confessing that they deserve to die, they are making confession of their sin; they are repentant"

And now look, John is baptizing, and Jesus comes; and when John gives the call for repentant sinners to come down to be baptized, Jesus walks down to the Jordan, and John says, "O Lord, not this, I cannot baptize You: I have need to be baptized of Thee, and comest Thou to me?" It is as though he would say, "I am baptizing sinners; You are not a sinner. I cannot baptize You. I am a sinner; You might well baptize me, but it is not for me to baptize You." But Jesus said, You "suffer it to be so now: for thus it becometh us to fulfil all righteousness." What did He mean by that? It is just as if He said: "What you say is perfectly true; I am not a sinner, I have nothing to repent of, but I am going to fulfil every righteous demand of God, and I want you to let Me be baptized with them, because I am taking the sinner's place." In other words, He says to the Father, "I am not going to plead My goodness to Thee as an exemption from death, but My goodness I present on behalf of others and I am going to die for them." Those are the people in whom He delights, those who confess their sins. Some have an idea that saints are people who have no sins to confess. But it is the very opposite. Saints are those who come before God confessing their sins, and He constitutes them saints. I plead My goodness, says He, not on My own account, "but to the saints that are in the earth, and to the excellent, in whom is all My delight"

And in the next verse He contrasts the people who turn away from God with them that walk in obedience to the Word of God. "Their sorrows shall be multiplied that hasten after another god." How we need to remember that today. Well, you say, we do not go to other gods now. We know too much. I do not bow down to gods of gold, stone or brass or iron. But anything you put in the place of God Himself, anything you allow to dominate or control your life short of God Himself, is another god. Self is another god; money is another god when it takes the place of God; fame is another idol; and love is another. I have known some cases of the last named. I get lots of queer letters. A man wrote me like this: "My dear pastor: I want your advice. I am interested in a divorced lady whom I intend to marry, and I would like to know if it is scriptural." And then in writing him I said, "What difference does it make to you whether it is scriptural or not, if you intend to marry her anyway? And yet you write to me for advice." They make up their minds they are going to do a certain thing, and these things become gods that they worship. What is the result? Nobody ever yet found peace of mind or joy of heart by going after anything that is contrary to the mind of God. Their sorrows shall be multiplied that hasten after another god.

And now, says the Lord Jesus, "Their drink offerings of blood will I not offer, nor take up their names into My lips." I will never put anything before My soul but My Father God. "The Lord," that is, Jehovah, "is the portion of Mine inheritance and of My cup." You love the twenty-third Psalm, do you not? Do you know the real speaker in the twenty-third Psalm is the Lord Jesus Christ? You say, "The Lord is my Shepherd." But Jesus said, "Jehovah is My Shepherd; I shall not want." And it was Jesus who said, "Yea, though I walk through the valley of the shadow of death, I will fear no evil; for Thou art with Me." And He went to the Cross. It is Jesus who said in that Psalm, "My cup runneth over." "Jehovah is the portion of Mine inheritance and of My cup." Now connect the twenty-third Psalm with it. "My cup runneth over." If you can say, "Jehovah is the portion of my cup," you will soon be able to say, "My cup runneth over." You begin to apprehend something of God's wonderful love and grace, and your cup will soon be filled right up and running over.

"Thou maintainest My lot." You know when Israel came out of Egypt, God gave them different lots for their inheritance. What was Jesus' lot? The lot of perfect subjection to the Father's will. "Thou maintainest My lot. The lines are fallen unto Me in pleasant places; yea, I have a goodly heritage." Who said this? The Man who is called the Man of Sorrows. Did it ever strike you in this way? As you read those four Gospels you never have the account of the life of a sad Man. He was characteristically a Man of gladness; He was a joyful Man but not a jolly one. You know there are some of us who either go down into the dumps or else we go over to the other side, and we become clowns and buffoons and are real jolly. But He was a glad Man, a joyful Man, a peaceful Man, because He was a Man living in fellowship with the Father, and all the sorrows He had to go through could not interfere in any way with His Father's love.

"I will bless the Lord, who hath given Me counsel." In the book of the prophet Isaiah we read, "He wakeneth morning by morning, He wakeneth Mine ear to hear as the learned" (50:4). What do I learn from that? I learn that my blessed Lord as a Man here on earth studied His Bible every day, and every morning He got something fresh from it. He was a normal Child and a normal young Man and a normal mature Man. He was getting something from God every day, and He was passing it on to others. I learned years ago that if I am to be of any use to others, I must go quietly before Him and let Him open my eyes, let Him tell me something of His secrets, and when the time comes I will have something to pass on to other people. That is what our Saviour did. He learned from the Father. They are the words that the Father gives Him. What perfect subjection! "I will bless the Lord, who hath given Me counsel: My reins also instruct Me in the night seasons." In other words, my inward being shall instruct me during the night seasons. The blessed Lord had many a sleepless night out there on the mountainside, alone with the Father. He knew what was before Him. He was the only Man in all Israel that understood the significance of all the sacrificial system. He could look at the Temple, He could see that sacrifice on the altar, and He knew He was the true Lamb of sacrifice. He could watch the passover lamb and knew it typified Himself. He could read the Word and He knew that all the Word had to do with Him. Just think what it was to Jesus to ponder over Isaiah 53, "He was wounded for our transgressions," and to know that all applied to Him.

But now see the perfection of His obedience. "I have set the Lord always before Me." The best I can say after half a century of service is, "I have set Jehovah sometimes before me." I wish I had done it more. But to be able to say what He said, "I have set Jehovah always before me," I have never had any other motive than to please Him, I have never had any other thought than to honor Him, we cannot say that. But here was One whose heart was perfect. The One who can say, "I have set the Lord always before Me," can say in perfect confidence, "because He is at My right hand, I shall not be moved." God was at His right hand before Herod, before Caiaphas, and even when the face of God had been hidden from Him on Calvary, still God always was at His right hand.

Now notice how He can look at the Cross. He knows all the anguish of the Cross, but He goes to that Cross in perfect confidence, knowing that He is coming through in triumph. "Therefore My heart is glad, and My glory rejoiceth." He is speaking of His tongue. Now James calls the tongue a deadly evil. David calls his tongue a glory. The tongue is a glory when it is used to bless the Lord. "My flesh also shall rest in hope." I will go into that tomb in perfect confidence, knowing that Thou wilt raise Me up. "For Thou wilt not leave My soul in hell." The word translated "hell" means Hades. It is the place for disembodied spirits between death and resurrection, that is, the unseen world. But He says, "Thou wilt not leave My soul in Hades, neither wilt Thou suffer Thine Holy One to see corruption." "My soul," that is the inward man. His body will not be allowed to corrupt He knew that His Father would bring Him back from the dead. "Neither wilt Thou suffer Thine Holy One to see corruption." This (illegible) not refer to David, though David wrote it. David has not been raised; his body corrupted. But great David's greater Son, our Lord Jesus, never saw corruption. And so, looking on to resurrection, He said, "Thou wilt shew Me the path of life," that is, resurrection life: "in Thy presence is fulness of joy." He is looking on to the glorious ascension when He will take His place again at God's right hand in heaven. "At Thy right hand there are pleasures for evermore." Those pleasures He lives to share with those who trust Him. What a difference between pleasures of sin and pleasures for evermore! "At [God's] right hand there are pleasures for evermore."

INTERCEDING WITH GOD
PSALM 17

WE HAVE NOTICED THAT IN THE EARLY PART OF THIS BOOK a great many of these Psalms have to do primarily with David's personal experiences. This particular Psalm evidently was written either during the time that he was fleeing from King Saul and his army or when he was hiding from the armies of his own son, Absalom. It probably has reference to the former case. One can understand how David would pen these words perhaps some night when he was restless, unable to sleep, on the alert, for he knew the enemy was pursuing him. He could not know the instant they might come upon him and an engagement be precipitated, for he realized that from the human standpoint he was in danger of his life every moment. In such circumstances he turned to God. To whom else could he turn?

How wonderfully these Psalms fit in to similar conditions in the lives of God's beloved people. How much they meant to the suffering in Israel during the days of the Maccabees when they were being so cruelly hunted down and slain, save as God put His hand upon Judas Maccabee and enabled them to defeat the army of the Syrians. And how much they have meant to Christian sufferers during all the centuries whether persecuted by pagan Rome and other heathen powers, or whether in the case of Protestants suffering at the hands of an apostate church because of their faithfulness to the Word of God and the gospel of His grace, or whether, as in the case of the Covenanters of Scotland when the ruling powers were seeking to force upon Christian people a religious system that they could not conscientiously accept, and they too were hunted like partridges on the mountains and never knew what day the heather would be stained with their blood.

But we do not see all that is in these Psalms if we think of them merely as presenting the experiences of David or of other believers who like him have been suffering from human foes. We need to go deeper than that, we need to remember that David was, after all, a typical character. In very large measure he typified our Lord Jesus Christ. His very name is significant. The word "David" means "The beloved," and God the Father said of our blessed Lord Jesus, "This is My beloved Son [this is My David] in whom I am well pleased" (Matt. 3:17). One of the earliest incidents recorded in the life of David was when he came from his father's house in order to minister to his brethren who were in suffering and distress in the war with the Philistines. He reminds us of the Lord who came from His Father's house of glory with arms full of blessing for His needy people in this world. And again, David's city is significant. He belonged to Bethlehem, and our blessed Saviour was born in that city. The name too is significant, Bethlehem, "The house of bread." But it never really answered to its name until Jesus was born there. He says, "I am the bread which came down from heaven" (John 6:41). And then how wonderfully David typified our blessed Lord Jesus Christ in his rejection. The very people that he benefited the most turned upon him with hatred and bitterness. And so our Lord Jesus Christ had to know all the bitterness, the hatred, the untrustworthiness of the hearts of those whom He came to save, and at last He went to the Cross and there gave Himself in sacrifice for our redemption. So as we read these Psalms we need to listen carefully to hear, not merely the voice of David, but the voice of Jesus.

I do not know a word in this Psalm that may not have been uttered to the Father by our blessed Lord on one of those nights when out on the mountainside communing with Him, for we may be very sure that He largely used the words of Holy Scripture. What we especially see in this seventeenth Psalm is the righteous man sustained by the Word in the midst of his enemies, and surely that was the case with our blessed Lord Jesus Christ. There is one thing in regard to the mystery of the incarnation that we need to lay hold on and it is this: though our Lord was both God and Man in one blessed, adorable Person, from the moment that He came into this world until that moment when He cried, "Father, into Thy hands I commend My spirit" (Luke 23:46), He chose not to act as God, though He was God, but He chose to act as a Man of faith dependent in every respect upon the Father's will and guided by the Holy Spirit. It is difficult for us to understand how He who was God and Man could become so utterly will-less in this scene that the Father's will was the only will He knew. And the Father's will was expressed in the Holy Scriptures which He studied from a Child and was manifested by the Holy Spirit who dominated and controlled the Man Christ Jesus. You remember when He went into the wilderness after His baptism, Scripture says, "Then was Jesus led up of the Spirit into the wilderness to be tempted of the devil" (Matt. 4:1). One of the evangelists uses a stronger word; he says He was driven of the Spirit into the wilderness (Mark 1:12). He was absolutely under the control of the Holy Spirit of God. Man had so terribly dishonored God, there had been such grave rebellion against His will all down through the years that our Lord Jesus Christ, before He went to the Cross to settle the sin question, made it the business of His life to glorify the Father fully by giving Him here on earth a human life that was absolutely yielded to Him. In connection with the incarnation we need to remember that our blessed Lord was just as truly God as if He had never become man, and He was as truly man as if He had never been God, but His manhood was never separated from His deity. Nevertheless, in this scene He chose to act as man and not simply as God. The Man Christ Jesus, as to the mystery of His Person, is God over all blessed forevermore, but He acted here before the Father as a dependent man. How beautifully that comes out in this Psalm. We can hear Him, as it were, speaking to His Father when foes are pressing about Him, when He is met with rejection on every hand, when for the love of His heart He is receiving only hatred.

"Hear the right, O Lord, attend unto My cry, give ear unto My prayer, that goeth not out of feigned lips." What a word this is for us. It is so possible for prayer to go out of feigned lips; it is so possible to pray absolutely beyond our experience. Have you ever heard people pray something like this, "O Lord, we do thank Thee for Thy wondrous love and grace, for the way Thou dost so fully satisfy our hearts," and then the next night, perhaps, they are off to the world for satisfaction. That is prayer going out of feigned lips. Or, have you ever heard people pray like this, "O Lord, grant that the love of Christ may absolutely control us, that nothing but His grace and love toward others may be seen," and within twenty minutes they are saying the meanest, unkindest things about fellow believers or about others in the world? That is prayer going out of feigned lips. Sometimes people pray like this, "O Lord, we look up to Thee. We trust Thee for everything, for daily bread to meet our need," and yet within an hour they may be talking to you about their circumstances and saying, "I am nearly worried to death; I don't know what I am going to do." The two things do not go together. That is praying out of feigned lips. But the Lord Jesus could say, "Give ear unto My prayer, that goeth not out of feigned lips." His inmost being was in full accord with the words of His mouth.

There is a beautiful figure of that in connection with the Tabernacle. Every whit of it uttered His glory. Surrounding the court of that tabernacle there were curtains of fine twined linen suspended from pillars, forming the wall, all around it. That speaks of Christ's righteousness before the world. The world from the outside could see that white curtain surrounding the court, and the white linen always speaks of righteousness in Scripture. But inside where the sanctuary itself stood there were ten curtains of fine twined linen fastened together that formed the tent of the tabernacle, the tabernacle proper. The world outside could not see those curtains for they were covered over with goats' hair and rams' skins dyed red and seal skins, or badgers' skins curtains. They were there for the priests and for God to see. But do you get this point? If you were outside you saw the curtains of fine twined linen surrounding the court, and as God looked down He saw the curtains of fine twined linen inside the sanctuary. In other words, the Lord Jesus Christ's righteousness was just the same under the eye of God as it was under the eye of man. It is so different with us. We can often seem so righteous and so good and so holy before our brethren, but as God looks down upon us it is so different. There was nothing like that with Jesus. In every respect His inward life and His outward life were in perfect agreement. He was just the same before men that He was before God. He was just the same in the presence of God that He was in the presence of men, and that is why He could say, "Give ear unto My prayer, that goeth not out of feigned lips." There was nothing unreal about Jesus. Oh, that we might be more like Him!

"Let My sentence come forth from Thy presence." That is another way of saying, "I just hand My case over to Thee; whatever Thou dost choose will be all right." "Let My sentence come forth from Thy presence; let Thine eyes behold the things that are equal." "I know Thou wilt weigh everything right, Father, and so I hand it over to Thee." And then He can say, "Thou hast proved Mine heart; Thou hast visited Me in the night; Thou hast tried Me, and shalt find nothing; I am purposed that My mouth shall not transgress." He was the holy, sinless Saviour! He had to be that or He never could have died for me. If there had been any evil way in Him, He would have needed a Saviour Himself, but because He was ever the Holy Son of God, He was competent to take my sin upon Himself and die in my room and stead.

Now notice the place the Word of God had in His life, "Concerning the works of men, by the word of Thy lips I have kept Me from the paths of the destroyer." Thou hast held fast "My goings in Thy paths, that My footsteps slip not." The Lord Jesus Christ who was the Eternal Word, and He was the theme of all Holy Scripture, chose as a Man on earth to live by the Word. He fed on the Word; He was sustained by the Word. When Satan said, "If Thou be the Son of God, command that these stones be made bread" (Matt. 4:3), He met him with the Word and said, "It is written, Man shall not live by bread alone, but by every word that proceedeth out of the mouth of God" (Matt. 4:4). And so He met the devil in one temptation after another with the Word, for the Word was hidden in His heart and there was no possibility of His sinning against the Father. Would that you and I were more controlled by the Word. So often we think of it as something to exercise our minds about, and we are more concerned about getting an intellectual understanding of Scripture than we are of hiding the Word in our hearts. That is why we are so ready to run to hear all kinds of thrilling addresses and why we spend so little time over the Word privately and why we care so little whether we get to hear the Word if it is simply the opening up of the truth for our practical sanctification. As far as the private life is concerned there are some who seldom open a Bible from one week to another. The blessed Lord could say, "He wakeneth morning by morning, He wakeneth Mine ear to hear as the learned" (Isa. 50:4). Think of Him, the holy, spotless Son of God, feeding on the Word, and yet you and I imagine we can get along without it! God give us a deeper love for the Word of God and help us to eat it that we too may say, "Concerning the works of men, by the word of Thy lips I have kept Me from the paths of the destroyer."

And then notice His perfect confidence in the Father, in verses 6 and 7, "I have called upon Thee, for Thou wilt hear Me, O God: incline Thine ear unto Me, and hear My speech. Shew Thy marvelous loving-kindness, O Thou that savest by Thy right hand them which put their trust in Thee from those that rise up against them." Is it not lovely to listen, as it were, to the secret things going on between the Father and the Son, the things that the Lord Jesus delighted to say to His Father when He was alone with Him, for that is what you have in a Psalm like this.

How beautiful the next verse is, "Keep me as the apple of the eye, hide me under the shadow of Thy wings." These two figures are used frequently in the Old Testament. "The apple of the eye." If you were to look up that word "apple" in a critical concordance or a Hebrew lexicon you might be surprised at the real word, for the literal Hebrew is, "little man"—"Keep me as the little man in the eye." If you stand close to me and you look into my eye, what do you see there? A little man and that little man is yourself; you see yourself reflected upside down; you are a little man in my eye. Now the Lord Jesus says to the Father, David says to Jehovah, "Keep me as the little man in Thine eye." God is always looking at you, and you are reflected in His eye. How deep is His interest in you! And then the other figure is that of a great eagle protecting its young. "Hide Me under the shadow of Thy wings." "He that dwelleth in the secret place of the most High shall abide under the shadow of the Almighty" (Psa. 91:1). "From the wicked that oppress me, from my deadly enemies, who compass me about."

In verses 10 to 15 you find again contrasted the men of the world and the man of faith. He describes the men of the world, men who live for self, "They are inclosed in their own fat: with their mouth they speak proudly." They are haughty men, they are enemies of righteousness. "They have now compassed us in our steps: they have set their eyes bowing down to the earth." They are like their master, for "The devil, as a roaring lion, walketh about, seeking whom he may devour" (1 Pet. 5:8). "Like as a lion that is greedy of his prey, and as it were a young lion lurking in secret places. Arise, O Lord, disappoint [hinder] him." It is really little more than "hinder," it means to get there first before the enemy can do anything. "Cast him down." But notice how he speaks of these wicked men, "Deliver my soul from the wicked, which is Thy sword. From the men which are Thy hand." One reason God tolerates wicked men in the world instead of sending them to hell is that He uses them as His scourge for the righteous when they need a whipping. That is why the prophet calls them, 'Thy sword." You remember God said that He raised up Nebuchadnezzar to come against the people to punish them. He uses the ungodly to test, to try, and to restrain His own people.

These "men of the world," "have their portion in this life." It is like those of whom we read in The Revelation. Frequently in that book we read of "them that dwell upon the earth." That does not mean people living in this world, but people who have refused the heavenly calling and have their portion down here. They are all about us; they have no interest in heaven; they have no interest in God or His Christ. The only world they care anything about is this world. They "have their portion in this life." And so they are satisfied with children. The word "full" really means "satisfied." That is, when a man accumulates a great fortune he says, "I will pass it on to them," and he just lives on in his children. But with the righteous, how different! They are willing to lay down their lives for the blessing of others if need be. As for these men of the world they leave their substance to their children and do not know what is going to become of it.

But see the contrast. David says, in verse 15, "As for me, I will behold Thy face in righteousness: I shall be satisfied, when I awake, with Thy likeness." There are three passages in the book of Psalms that I love to link together. They are Psalm 18:30, "As for God, His way is perfect"; Psalm 103:15, "As for man, his days are as grass"; Psalm 17:15, "As for me, I will behold Thy face in righteousness: I shall be satisfied, when I awake, with Thy likeness." Notice these three statements, "As for God—as for man—as for me." "As for God, His way is perfect." No matter what comes I know He makes no mistake. Sickness may come, financial trouble may come, family trouble may come, church troubles may come—and there is no trouble on earth so bad as trouble among the people of God—but no matter what happens, "As for God, His way is perfect." As for man: David says, I have learned not to expect much from him, "his days are as grass." But "As for me, … I shall be satisfied, when I awake, with Thy likeness."

THE POWER OF HIS RESURRECTION
PSALM 18

THIS IS ANOTHER OF THE PSALMS OF DAVID WHICH UNDOUBTEDLY sets before us in a very wonderful way some personal experiences which he passed through during those dark and difficult years when he was hunted by King Saul like a partridge on the mountains, when at times he despaired of his own life, and became so discouraged that he felt there was no help for him; but eventually in his greatest distress he looked up and realized that God was for him. While this Psalm, like so many others, sets forth experiences that David passed through, as we read it in the light of New Testament revelation we can see that the Spirit of Christ was speaking through David. Of course David himself was a sinful man and therefore when he speaks he necessarily says some things as he makes confession of his sins to God that our Lord Jesus Christ could not say, for He had no sin to confess. But on the other hand, when he speaks of his rejection, of the way he was spurned and set aside, hunted almost to death by his brethren whom he loved, and then when he tells of Jehovah's marvelous deliverance, it is not hard to see that David was a typical person and that his life and experiences set forth something of the life and experiences of our Lord Jesus Christ.

In these opening verses, as so often is the case in the Psalms, he gives us the consummation in the very beginning. He writes because his heart is overflowing with gratitude to God for His goodness. "I will love Thee, O Lord, my strength," he exclaims. And then notice the many different figures of speech he uses in verse 2 to express his confidence in God. "The Lord is my rock, and my fortress, and my deliverer, my God, my strength, in whom I will trust; my buckler, and the horn of my salvation, and my high tower." That expression, "The horn of my salvation," may not be so clear to us as it would be to those who lived in the time that David wrote. The horn refers to the horns of the cattle on Lebanon, and it is used frequently in the Old Testament for a symbol of strength or of power. Think of one of those mighty bulls of Bashan pushing his way through all opposition with those great horns of his. David says, "The Lord … is the horn of my salvation"—the strength of my salvation—"and my high tower." I think you can get the picture if you think of a vast stony mountain rising up from the plain, right on the top of it a fortress, and at one corner of this a high tower and the enemy on the plain below. David says, "The Lord is my rock, and my fortress, and my deliverer." And He gives all that is needed for furnishing by the way.

Years ago while working among the Laguna Indians, we were asked to speak at a little village called Pawate. We rode in large wagons drawn by horses (for it was in the days before automobiles) for some fourteen miles over rough roads until we reached this village. We had a meeting in the afternoon, and Indians from all about gathered. We started back at 4:30 or 5:00 o'clock because we were to have a meeting at Casablanca that night. We had not gone very far when we saw a terrible storm was evidently to break over us. Soon we could see that the rain was pouring down at a distance and driving rapidly toward us. I said, "We are certainly going to get soaked." Our driver replied, "I hope not, I think we can make the rock before the storm reaches us. There is a great rock ahead and if we can make it we will be sheltered." We hurried on and soon saw a vast rock rising up from the plain, perhaps forty or fifty feet in height, covering possibly an acre or more of ground. As we drew near we saw a great cave going right into the rock. Instead of stopping to unhitch the horses, our driver drove right into the cave and in another minute or two the storm broke over the rock in all its fury. The storm raged outside and one of the Indians struck up in the Laguna tongue, "Rock of Ages cleft for me, let me hide myself in Thee," and we realized the meaning of the poet's words then as perhaps never before. I think David had something like that in mind. "The Lord is my rock."

Then if you think of a great fortress above and a high tower on top of that you get the finished picture. The thought, of course, is that no matter what my circumstances may be, no matter what danger may threaten, the Lord is the all sufficient One. If you put your trust in Him, you will never be frightened any more. It is a great thing to be able to say, "I will trust, and not be afraid" (Isa. 12:2). When we get so terrified because of circumstances, when so depressed because of conditions, it shows that we are not really confiding in God. When our blessed Lord was here on earth, nothing ever ruffled His spirit until that awful hour when He was facing the sin question on our behalf, and He could not have been the Holy One of God if that had not distressed Him deeply. But all the shame men heaped on Him, all the suffering He had to bear, the forsaking of His own and the misrepresentations that were circulated, none of these things distressed Him because He was resting in the will of the Father, and if you and I want to be overcomers in hours of temptation and trial we need to rest in God, to find our refuge in the rock, the fortress, the high tower.

And so the Psalmist says, "I will call upon the Lord, who is worthy to be praised: so shall I be saved from mine enemies." And then he tells us of a very bitter experience he went through. With David it was this, he came near to death. He said on one occasion, "There is but a step between me and death" (1 Sam. 20:3), for he felt as though, humanly speaking, all hope was gone and he had to face the terrors of death. He was a young man when going through those sufferings. He was only thirty years old when he was crowned king at Hebron. And so he describes the terrible condition of mind as he was facing death, and could see no way out until he called upon God, and then he depicts in graphic language the way God set all heaven, as it were, in motion for the deliverance of His afflicted child. David came near to death, and God delivered him; our blessed Lord Jesus Christ went down into death, and it was death under the divine judgment, the judgment due to sin, and that made it unspeakably awful to Him, but He went down into death with absolute confidence that God, His Father, was going to bring Him up out of it. I think we may see in this Psalm something of the power of His Resurrection, of which we read in the Epistle to the Ephesians, chapter 1, verse 19, where the apostle prays that the saints may know "what is the exceeding greatness of His [God's] power to us-ward who believe, according to the working of His mighty power, Which He wrought in Christ, when He raised Him from the dead, and set Him at His own right hand in the heavenly places." It was a mighty act of power when God brought Christ up from the dead and then set Him at His own right hand, "Far above all principality, and power, and might, and dominion." These are different names for hosts of angels, some good, some evil. "And every name that is named, not only in this world, but also in that which is to come."

Then look at Philippians 2. After we read of the humiliation of Christ, of the depths into which He descended, we read in verse 9, "Wherefore God also hath highly exalted Him, and given Him a name which is above every name: That at the name of Jesus every knee should bow, of things in heaven, and things in earth, and things under the earth; And that every tongue should confess that Jesus Christ is Lord, to the glory of God the Father." All created beings have to recognize the power and majesty of God that raised Christ from the dead and set Him at His own right hand.

Then turn to the Epistle to the Colossians, chapter 2, verses 13 and 14, where we read of His death on the Cross, "And you, being dead in your sins and the uncircumcision of your flesh, hath He quickened together with Him, having forgiven you all trespasses; Blotting out the handwriting of ordinances that was against us, which was contrary to us, and took it out of the way, nailing it to His cross." And in verse 15 we read, "And having spoiled principalities and powers, He made a shew of them openly, triumphing over them in it." These are evil principalities and evil powers, hosts of wicked angels, fallen angels—"Having spoiled [made a prey of] principalities and powers, He made a shew of them openly, triumphing over them in it." See how graphically David depicts this. Remember, the word "David" means "Beloved" and he is here a type of Christ, God's beloved, going down into the sorrows of death. Verse 4, "The sorrows of death compassed me, and the floods of ungodly men made me afraid. The sorrows of hell [of Sheol, of the unseen world] compassed me about: the snares of death prevented me. In my distress I called upon the Lord, and cried unto my God." Think of the blessed Lord hanging on the Cross and seeing before Him the awful pit into which men must go who reject His grace, and in His infinite loving kindness to sinners He goes down into that pit Himself.

> "The heavens are clothed with shades of night
> While Jesus doth with demons fight."

And there on the Cross He faces death in all its terribleness as an expression of the judgment of God against sin, but He commits His soul to the Father. "Father, into Thy hands I commend My spirit" (Luke 23:46).

"He heard My voice out of His temple, and My cry came before Him, even into His ears." Surely you have never found in Scripture a more remarkable description of God acting in omnipotent power to bring Christ back from death than you get in these verses. "Then the earth shook and trembled; the foundations also of the hills moved and were shaken, because He was wroth." We read in the New Testament that there was a great earthquake "And the graves were opened" (Matt. 27:52). "There went up a smoke out of His nostrils, and fire out of His mouth devoured: coals were kindled by it." Listen to this, "He bowed the heavens also, and came down: and darkness was under His feet." It is God descending in power to raise His Son from the dead. "He rode upon a cherub, and did fly: yea, He did fly upon the wings of the wind. He made darkness His secret place; His pavilion round about Him were dark waters and thick clouds of the skies. At the brightness that was before Him His thick clouds passed, hail stones and coals of fire. The Lord also thundered in the heavens, and the Highest gave His voice; hail stones and coals of fire. Yea, He sent out His arrows, and scattered them; and He shot out lightnings, and discomfited them." Scattered whom? If you had been there that day when the blessed Christ of God lay in the tomb, you would have seen those soldiers on guard, and away off in the distance you would have seen the frightened groups of His disciples wondering what would happen next; but if your eyes had been opened, you might have seen hosts of wicked spirits, principalities and powers, Satan, the prince of the power of the air, all those hosts of wicked spirits hovering about that tomb saying, "He must never come out. We have Him now where we want Him." It was the hour of Satan's triumph, but see what happened.

"Yea, He sent out His arrows, and scattered them; and He shot out lightnings, and discomfited them. Then the channels of waters were seen, and the foundations of the world were discovered at Thy rebuke, O Lord, at the blast of the breath of Thy nostrils. He sent from above, He took me, He drew me out of many waters. He delivered me from may strong enemy, and from them which hated me: for they were too strong for me. They prevented me in the day of my calamity: but the Lord was my stay." Can you not see that David was picturing his experiences before his death, while this is a picture of our blessed Lord after He died, when omnipotent power raised Him from the dead? "He drew me out of many waters"—many waters of death. He was raised up by infinite power, and now as the risen One He begins to speak. Verse 19, "He brought Me forth also into a large place: He delivered Me, because He delighted in Me." What else could God do when His blessed Son had settled the sin question, when He met every claim that divine righteousness had against guilty men, what else could God do but express His delight in His Son by raising Him from the dead?

"The Lord rewarded me according to my righteousness; according to the cleanness of my hands hath He recompensed me. For I have kept the ways of the Lord, and have not wickedly departed from my God. For all His judgments were before me, and I did not put away His statutes from me. I was also upright before Him, and I kept myself from mine iniquity." David could not fully enter into all this. David, even in those days fleeing from Saul, often failed. How perfidiously he acted in the court of the Philistines, how he lost his temper in connection with the bad treatment that he received from Nabal and was only prevented from wreaking a fierce vengeance by the intercession of Abigail. But the One of whom he was a type was the sinless One who could say, "The Lord rewarded Me according to My righteousness." Of course as far as doing any harm to King Saul was concerned, David could say, "The Lord rewarded me according to my righteousness; according to the cleanness of my hands hath He recompensed me. For I have kept the ways of the Lord, and have not wickedly departed from my God." But it is the Lord Jesus Christ who comes before us here as the absolutely righteous One, the One whom God exalted to His own right hand after He settled the sin question.

And now he sets forth the principles of divine government, in verses 24 to 30. "Therefore hath the Lord recompensed Me according to My righteousness, according to the cleanness of My hands in His eyesight. With the merciful Thou wilt shew Thyself merciful; with an upright man Thou wilt shew Thyself upright; With the pure Thou wilt shew Thyself pure; and with the froward Thou wilt shew Thyself froward." Here are principles that we may well take to heart. Do you sometimes feel as though God is not treating you quite as you deserve? You may not say it in so many words, but have you not felt that way? I have had people say, "I do not understand why God allowed this or that to come upon me. I am not conscious of any wrongdoing." Or some may say, "I do not understand why people treat me as they do." Here is what the Word says, "With the merciful thou wilt shew thyself merciful." Jesus said, "Blessed are the merciful: for they shall obtain mercy" (Matt. 5:7). Do you know why God seems to be so hard on some of us? It is because we are so hard on other people. We judge so severely; we are so critical of other folk. As a rule people who are the most sensitive to criticism are those who are the most ready to criticize other folk God is taking note of how we treat other people, and He is treating us in measure according to that. "With an upright man Thou wilt shew Thyself upright." In other words, God will undertake for the upright man. "With the pure Thou wilt shew Thyself pure; and with the forward"—that is, the self-willed—God will seem to show Himself self-willed. That is, He will visit chastisement upon the self-willed.

"For Thou wilt save the afflicted people; but wilt bring down high looks." If I want the favor of God, I must be sure that I am taking a lowly place before Him. As long as I justify myself, God can only condemn me but when I condemn myself, then God is there to justify me.

"For Thou wilt light my candle: the Lord my God will enlighten my darkness." No matter what the gloom around, faith can look up to Him and can count on Him to give the needed light. "For by thee I have run through a troop; and by my God have I leaped over a wall." He just imagines himself as one man with a great troop of the enemy before him but he fixes his heart on God and in perfect confidence in Him runs through them. Or, he sees a great wall around him, and they are hemming him in, and he says, "By my God have I leaped over a wall." Faith just counts on God as the Deliverer. You remember what God said to Israel, "If you walk with Me, obey My word, one of you shall chase a thousand and two of you shall put ten thousand to flight." And so we need never be afraid of the foe as long as we are really going on in fellowship with God.

Then we have that beautiful word, "As for God, His way is perfect: the word of the Lord is tried: He is a buckler to all those that trust in Him." Would it not be well if we all had this firmly implanted in our souls—God never makes any mistakes? Sometimes you have had an idea that He has made a few mistakes in connection with you; deep in your heart you have felt it but faith can stand with David and say, "As for God, His way is perfect." Never any mistake. I may not understand the why of a great many experiences that God permits me to go through, but I will by and by.

> *"When I stand with Christ on high,*
> *Looking o'er life's history,*
> *Then, dear Lord, shall I fully know,*
> *Not till then, how much I owe."*

And I will realize that all God's ways with me were in perfect love and righteousness.

And now in the verses that immediately follow you have once more an expression of faith, of the Messiah in the days of His humiliation. "For who is God save the Lord? or who is a rock save our God? It is God that girdeth me with strength, and maketh my way perfect." What had he said before? "As for God, His way is perfect" but if I walk in fellowship with God, "It is God that maketh *my* way perfect." "He maketh my feet like hinds' feet [that is, deer's feet] and setteth me upon my high places." These particular hinds were found on the mountains. They were very sure footed and would leap from crag to crag. David says, "He maketh my feet like hinds' feet, and setteth me upon my high places." It is a great thing to have the faith that enables us to surmount the difficulties and rise above the mistakes of earth.

And then when we have to meet the foe, "He teacheth my hands to war, so that a bow of steel is broken by mine arms. Thou hast also given me the shield of Thy salvation: and Thy right hand hath holden me up." And now, is not this the spirit of Christ speaking through David, "And Thy gentleness hath made me great"? Who but Jesus could say that in all its fullness? And He says to us, "Take My yoke upon you, and learn of Me; for I am meek and lowly in heart: and ye shall find rest unto your souls" (Matt. 11:29). We miss it so when we become so dignified and stern and hard in our ways with people. The Lord Jesus conquered by gentleness. "Thy gentleness hath made me great." I picked up an old book in Canada one time, a history of the world, written back in the sixteenth century, printed in Old English type. I was thumbing through it, and I came down to the beginning of the Christian era and saw these words, "It was in these days that that goodly Gentleman, Jesus Christ, was born in Bethlehem of Judea." I said to myself, "Dear me, I never heard Him spoken of like that before." It gave me a shock for a moment, and then the next moment I thought, but what better term could describe Him, "That goodly Gentleman"? A Gentleman? What do you mean by that term? The idea some people have of a gentleman is a man that does not work for a living. But a gentleman is a gentle man, a man who is considerate of other people. If you want to be recognized as a gentleman, you must learn to be considerate of other people. When I was a boy my mother used to tell me that politeness is doing or saying the kindest thing in the kindest way. That is what Jesus did. "Thy gentleness hath made me great."

"Thou hast enlarged my steps under me, that my feet did not slip. I have pursued mine enemies, and overtaken them: neither did I turn again till they were consumed." David is speaking here of having triumphed and instead of fleeing from his enemies they are fleeing from him. The spiritual foes are now fleeing from the Lord Jesus. "I have wounded them that they were not able to rise: they are fallen under my feet. For Thou hast girded me with strength unto the battle: Thou hast subdued under me those that rose up against me."

And then look at verse 43 where we have a prophetic picture of our blessed Lord as Head of the new creation and Head over all the world when He reigns in power. "Thou hast delivered Me from the strivings of the people; and Thou hast made Me the head of the heathen [of the nations]." Do not think that the word "heathen" always means idolaters. Our word was originally heath-men, men who lived in the wild places as contrasted with the cities. In other words, "Thou hast made Me the head of the Gentile nations," and some day He will be manifested as such. "A people whom I have not known shall serve Me." "He came unto His own, and His own received Him not" (John 1:11). "As soon as they hear of Me, they shall obey Me: the strangers shall submit themselves unto Me. The strangers shall fade away, and be afraid out of their close places. The Lord liveth; and blessed be My rock; and let the God of My salvation be exalted."

In the closing verses he comes back to that with which he began. He strikes again, as it were, the key note of absolute confidence in Jehovah. "It is God that avengeth Me, and subdueth the people under Me. He delivereth Me from Mine enemies: yea, Thou liftest Me up above those that rise up against Me: Thou hast delivered Me from the violent man. Therefore will I give thanks unto Thee, O Lord, among the heathen, and sing praises unto Thy name. Great deliverance giveth He to His king; and sheweth mercy to His anointed, to David, and to his seed for evermore." We know who His King is. David was a faint foreshadow of the true King. "And sheweth mercy to His anointed [His Messiah, the beloved] to David, and to his seed for evermore." David was promised that his seed should reign for ever and ever. The only way that could ever be is through David's Son triumphing over death, never to die again, and that is fulfilled in our Lord Jesus Christ.

THE TESTIMONY OF CREATION AND THE WORD OF GOD
PSALM 19

IN THIS NINETEENTH PSALM THE SPIRIT OF GOD CELEBRATES two things, draws our attention to two testimonies. First, in verses 1 to 6 we have the testimony to the majesty and power of God in creation. Then from verses 7 to 11 we have the testimony of the Word of God setting forth the divine purpose and counsels, making known the mind of God in respect to man. In verses 12 to 14 we have that exercise of soul which should result from a thoughtful consideration of these two testimonies.

There is no conflict whatever between the testimony of nature and the testimony of the Word of God. Men have often tried to put nature and the Bible in opposition the one to the other; have insisted that the Bible is not scientific and that science is not biblical. But the fact scientific and the truth biblical never contradict one another. The theories scientific, these scientific hypotheses that have never been proven, are often opposed to the revelation that God has given in His Word and true science is often opposed to certain interpretations which men have given to parts of the Bible. But real science is never opposed to a right understanding or a correct interpretation of the Bible because science is simply an orderly presentation of the facts of the natural universe, whereas the Bible is an orderly presentation of the mind of God in connection with redemption.

In the fourth and fifth chapters of the book of The Revelation you have a very wonderful contrast or comparison. In chapter 4, verse 3, you look into heaven and there you see One on the throne whose features are not plainly discerned. He dwells in such brilliant light that John himself could not distinguish His features. He says, "He that sat [on the throne] was to look upon like a jasper and a sardine stone." That is interesting because the jasper and the sardine were two of the stones that were on the breastplate of the high priest of old. They were the first and last stones mentioned. There were twelve stones on the breastplate arranged in four rows of three each, and on those twelve stones were graven the names of the tribes of Israel, and every one of those names has a definite meaning. The striking thing is that on the jasper stone was engraven the name "Reuben" and Reuben means, "Behold a son." On the sardius was engraven the name "Benjamin" and Benjamin means "Son of my right hand." John says, as it were, I could not see Him plainly, the glory was too brilliant. I could not discern His features, but I could see that He was like a jasper and a sardius stone. And then the four and twenty elders are seen falling down on their faces before Him that sat upon the throne, and they worshiped Him, we are told, that made heaven and earth and the sea and all the things which are therein. They worshiped the Son of God as the Creator of the material universe.

When you come to chapter five things become plainer, and John who has become accustomed to that brilliant glory now says, "I beheld, and, lo, in the midst of the throne … a Lamb as it had been slain" (verse 6), or as Weymouth's beautiful translation puts it, "I saw a Lamb that looked as though it had once been offered in sacrifice." There were the marks of death still upon the Lamb, and John says that "the four and twenty elders fell down before the Lamb" and they worshiped the Lamb and cried, "Thou art worthy … for Thou wast slain, and hast redeemed us to God by Thy blood out of every kindred, and tongue, and people, and nation; And hast made us unto our God a kingdom of priests" (verses 9, 10, 12). In chapter 4 you have the Lamb worshiped as Creator, and in chapter 5 He is worshiped as Redeemer. The poet has well said,

> "'Twas great to call a world from naught,
> 'Twas greater to redeem."

When we study the book of creation, when we look up into the heaven and look abroad over the earth, we find everywhere the evidences of divine power and might and wisdom. I cannot understand intelligent people questioning the reality or personality of God when they look out over this wonderful creation. If there were no mind behind this universe the suns and the starry systems would have long since crashed together and the universe would have gone to pieces; but the One who created the universe is "upholding all things by the word of His power" (Heb. 1:3). How strikingly the Psalmist stresses the being of God and the folly of questioning that reality, when He says, "He that planted the ear, shall He not hear? He that formed the eye, shall He not see?" (Psa. 94:9). Can you imagine any one with the ability to construct a human body, to bring a human body into existence and give it life, to construct an ear and make it possible for that ear to receive the sounds of the outside world, and yet that being know nothing about hearing himself? Can you imagine any one with wisdom enough to create an eye, that wonderful window of the soul, and yet not able to see himself? The very fact that we have such marvelous faculties is the proof that there must be a personal God behind this universe.

"The heavens declare the glory of God; and the firmament sheweth His handiwork." What is meant by "the heavens"? Not simply the sky but all those myriads upon myriads of orbs of light, stars, suns, moons, solar systems, one after another reaching out into infinity. There are no limits of space. That is one thing that it is absolutely impossible to think of; try as hard as you may and you cannot think of limited space. At once your mind says, I wonder what is on the other side. That limitless space is crowded with universes, many of them millions of times larger than ours. And all of these, the starry heavens, declare the glory of God—

> *"Forever singing as they shine*
> *'The hand that made us is divine.' "*

The first chapter of Genesis says, "In the beginning God created the heavens and the earth." Strange the stupid things that men will say. Only recently I ran up against the same old foolish statement that the first chapter of Genesis cannot be reliable because it tells of vegetation growing on the earth on the third day while the sun was not created until the fourth day, and you cannot have vegetation without sunlight; therefore it is absurd to think of trees growing before the sun was created. I grant that it is absurd, but the absurdity exists in the mind of the skeptic, not in the Word of God. The Word of God tells us that the sun was created before the days began. "In the beginning God created the heavens"—that takes in the sun—"and the earth"—these two terms take in all the orbs that roll through space. But when you come to the fourth day we read that the Lord God made the sun "to give light upon the earth." It does not say that He created the sun then, but up to that time the rays of the sun had not been focused upon the earth as they are now. There is no contradiction: the contradiction is only in the mind of the unbeliever. God, in the beginning, "created the heaven and the earth" and "the heavens declare the glory of God."

Have you noticed how the different orbs of the heavens are used as pictures of our Lord Jesus Christ and His redemptive work? For instance, He is called the "Sun of righteousness." He is called the "bright and morning star," and on the other hand, those who follow Him and do His bidding are to shine "as the stars for ever and ever." The moon is used as a picture of the people of God and the wonderful thing about the moon is that it has no light in itself, all its light is reflected glory. We, the people of God, have nothing in ourselves, we are darkness in ourselves but when brought to know the Sun of righteousness, we reflect His light. God uses these orbs of the heavens as pictures of His redemptive work.

"The heavens declare the glory of God; and the firmament sheweth His handiwork." What does he mean by the firmament? This involves another objection that I often run across, even in books, and it amazes me to think how foolish some men, wise in other respects, can be. Some of the great authorities perpetuate this same stupid thing, that the Hebrew people believed, and their Bible taught that just above the earth was a solid firmament and the sun, moon, and stars were set in that solid firmament. They say that now we know, of course, that this is not true and so we must discard the book of Genesis. What stupidity, what a blatant display of ignorance! When you turn to the first chapter of Genesis we read that the Lord God made the fowl to "fly above the earth in the open firmament of heaven" (verse 20). In a kind of crystal dome? No; the firmament is the atmosphere surrounding the earth. If the proportion of oxygen and nitrogen were changed, the whole universe would blow up. God has suspended this atmosphere around the earth and in the right proportions, so much oxygen and so much nitrogen, and therefore we are able to breathe, to exist, and if there were any marked change we would all die. And so "The firmament sheweth His handiwork." The firmament says, there is a God, there is a mind behind the universe. The chemist goes into his laboratory and takes so much oxygen and so much nitrogen, mixes them together and produces certain gases. I read of a professor of chemistry in San Jose, California, who some years ago, was giving some work in the laboratory and the students were mixing certain compounds, but they got things a little bit out of proportion and off it went and the whole side of the high school blew out. We would have that all the time if we did not have a God of absolute wisdom controlling the universe.

"Day unto day uttereth speech, and night unto night sheweth knowledge." In the daytime as we see the sun passing through the heavens, who can help but see that there must be a mind behind this universe that guides that sun and controls its movements? And when night comes and you look into the starry heaven, how can you help believing that there is a God who created all these things? And this is God's testimony to the heathen, who do not have any other witness, save that of conscience, to men who do not have the Bible.

"There is no speech nor language; Their voice is not heard." Notice how that should read. It says here in the A.V. "There is no speech nor language, where their voice is not heard," but the word "where" is in italics. What he is really saying is, if you want to hear the voice of God, if you want evidences of the reality of God, look up into the sky in the daytime and see the clouds, the sun, and the storms gathering, listen to the voice of the thunder, and then when night comes look upon the stars, those varied constellations, think how marvelously everything moves with exact mathematical precision. You will hear the voice of God, and yet there is no speech, their voice is not heard. But you cannot help, if you are thoughtful, but realize that there must be a divine mind behind the universe. And this testimony goes to all men everywhere.

"Their line is gone out through all the earth, and their words to the end of the world. In them hath He set a tabernacle for the sun, Which is as a bridegroom coming out of his chamber, and rejoiceth as a strong man to run a race." And is not this, after all, a picture of our Lord Jesus Christ? He is the Sun of Righteousness who by and by is to be revealed as the Bridegroom of His own, when He comes forth in power and glory to bless the whole universe, when that Sun of Righteousness arises "with healing in his wings" (Mal. 4:2). "His going forth is from the end of the heaven, and his circuit unto the ends of it: and there is nothing hid from the heat thereof." This is the testimony then of nature, and every man is responsible to heed that testimony. No honest man can look up into the heaven without the realization that there must be a God and without the realization that that God is a God of order, a God of righteousness. And what is righteousness? It is simply orderliness, and this universe is run in an orderly way, and therefore the testimony of the heavens is enough to convict a man of the need of repentance, of getting right with the God of the universe. But God has added more to that, He has given us His Word, and from verses 7 to 11 we have the testimony of the law.

"The law of the Lord is perfect, converting the soul." You will notice that the testimony of the law is given in a series of three couplets, three verses, and in each of these, two things are cited in order that we may consider them. Verse 7, "The law of the Lord is perfect, converting the soul: the testimony of the Lord is sure, making wise the simple." By this term "law" is not meant, of course, just the Ten Commandments. We think of them as the law of God, but by the law is meant the whole revelation of God's mind and will in His Word. In that sense the entire Word is the law of God, and this law is perfect. That is in accord with the New Testament revelation. "All scripture is given by inspiration of God, and is profitable for doctrine, for reproof, for correction, for instruction in righteousness: that the man of God may be perfect, throughly furnished unto all good works" (2 Tim. 3:16, 17). God has given a perfect revelation in His Word, and what is the effect if heeded? "Converting the soul," turning the soul to God. The Word of God, if received in the heart, if believed, turns the soul to God. Then note the second half of this couplet, "The testimony of the Lord is sure, making wise the simple." The word "testimony" again covers the whole Book. Do you want the wisdom that really counts? Study your Bible. How is it that men of the world who are wise as to other things are so ignorant as to spiritual things? It is because they ignore the testimony of the Word. "The testimony of the Lord is sure, making wise the simple." If you study your Bible in dependence upon the Holy Spirit you will find that it will give you an illumination, a knowledge, a wisdom that all the writings of men can never give you.

I have told elsewhere how, years ago when a young Salvation Army officer, I had come home for a brief furlough to southern California, where my folk had an olive ranch. I found an Irish preacher there, a poor man dying of tuberculosis, and he was too far gone for a change of climate to help him. He had asked to be allowed to live in a little tent away from the house and among the olive trees. There he had his bed and table and a chair, and when able to sit up, he sat there pondering over the Word of God and writing a few letters. When I came home my mother said, "I want you to go out there and see James Fraser." I went, and he greeted me very kindly and said, "Well, young man, you are trying to win souls," and he went on to give me a word of encouragement and then said, "Sit down and let me tell you a few things my Father has been saying to me."

Oh, the things he began to give me from the Word of God as I sat there for perhaps two hours. And then I said, "You must not talk any more, you will be exhausted."

He said, "Take these things and pass them on to others."

I said, "But how can I learn these things for myself? Can you tell me of some books I can read that will explain all these things?"

"My dear young man," he said, "I learned these things on my knees on the mud floor of a little thatched cottage in the north of Ireland with my open Bible on the chair before me. The One who wrote the Bible came day by day and explained them to me, and you can learn more in a few weeks on your knees, with God, over His Word than you can in all the schools in a lifetime."

I was amazed and I have thanked God all my life since for that little Irishman, James Fraser. All through the years I have cherished the lesson he taught me. If you want the wisdom that cometh from above, if you want knowledge that is real, study your Bible for yourself, in dependence upon the Holy Spirit of God. Do not just depend upon what others can give you. I am afraid there are many Christians who hardly ever open their Bibles except when they come to meeting. If we could only learn to spend time over the Book we would find the wisdom of God unfolded there.

Notice the second couplet in verse 8, "The statutes of the Lord are right, rejoicing the heart: the commandment of the Lord is pure, enlightening the eyes," This term "statutes" means, of course, the paths that God lays out for you, the instruction as to how you ought to walk People are sometimes afraid of God's statutes, but when you walk in them, instead of finding disappointment, your heart is filled with gladness. "The statutes of the Lord are right, rejoicing the heart: the commandment of the Lord is pure, enlightening the eyes." How different is God's working from man's imaginings. "God's simple unencumbered plan," so plain, so clear, enlightening the eyes! I have known men who were altogether unlettered and yet through the study of this Book, because they had learned in the school of God and His Word, they were wiser far than many who have had lots of degrees attached to the end of their names.

Then consider the last couplet in verse 9, "The fear of the Lord is clean, enduring for ever." It is not fear in the sense of being afraid of God but fear in the sense of standing in awe of His infinite holiness. As you read the Word and are brought consciously into His presence, that sense of awe comes over your soul and you say, I do not want to grieve a God like that; I want to walk in obedience to Him, and the result is the cleansing of your life. The things that you contract from the world around are cleansed out of your life. The other half of this couplet, "The judgments of the Lord [and it is not judgment in the sense of condemnatory judgment, but it is the decisions of the Lord] are true and righteous altogether." Do not ever believe anything else. Satan will try to make you think that the decisions of the Lord are often hard and cruel and will run contrary to your own best interests, but "The judgments [decisions] of the Lord are true and righteous altogether. More to be desired are they than gold, yea, than much fine gold: sweeter also than honey and the honeycomb." You begin to revel in this Word and you will say to yourself, I have never found anything so precious to my soul as this. Jeremiah said, "Thy words were found, and I did eat them; and Thy word was unto me the joy and rejoicing of mine heart" (Jer. 15:16). You remember what Job said, "I have esteemed the words of His mouth more than my necessary food" (Job 23:12). And here David adds his testimony and says, Thy truth is "more to be desired than gold, yea, than much fine gold: sweeter also than honey and the honeycomb."

"Moreover by them is thy servant warned." Study the Word of God not only for your own delight and upbuilding but also in order that you may be guarded from things contrary to the mind of God. John Bunyan wrote in the front of his Bible, "This Book will keep you from sin, or sin will keep you from this Book." If you are pondering over the Word of God day by day it will keep you from sin. If you are careless and cold of heart and out of fellowship with God, sin will keep you from the Book. "Moreover by them is Thy servant warned: and in keeping of them there is great reward." Keeping His Word unto the end.

From verses 12 to 14 we have the exercise of soul that is produced by pondering over the Word of God. The Psalmist asks, "Who can understand his errors?" I would have no way of testing myself if it were not for the Word. "Cleanse Thou me from secret faults." There are things in my life, every one of us can say, that nobody else knows anything about. God alone knows. Now, Lord, apply Thy Word and cleanse me from these hidden things, from secret faults. And he adds, "Keep back Thy servant also from presumptuous sins." What are presumptuous sins? He is distinguishing here presumptuous sins from sins of ignorance. Under the law there were no sacrifices for presumptuous sins—"The man that will do presumptuously, … shall die" (Deut. 17:12). The sacrifices were for sins of ignorance, "Keep back Thy servant from presumptuous sins." That is, wilful sins, direct violations of the revealed will of God. "Let them not have dominion over me: then shall I be upright, and I shall be innocent from the great transgression"—of violating the revealed will of God.

Now comes the closing prayer, and how aptly it fits the lips of every servant of Christ, yea, of every believer, but of every one in particular who seeks in any way to publicly serve God. "Let the words of my mouth, and the meditation of my heart, be acceptable in Thy sight, O Lord, my strength, and my redeemer." And if the words of my mouth, and the meditation of my heart, be acceptable to the Lord they must be in accordance with the Word. It is as one ministers the Word that he is acceptable to God.

PSALMS OF THE KINGDOM
PSALMS 20 AND 21

THUS FAR IN OUR ATTEMPT TO EXPOUND THIS PORTION of the Word of God I have not called attention to the beauties of some of these headings. For instance, Psalms 19, 20, and 21 are all headed alike, "To the chief Musician, A Psalm of David." Psalm 22 is also dedicated "To the chief Musician." But then you have a Hebrew term following that which is said to mean, "hind of the morning," referring to the antlers on the head of a deer as picturing the rays of the rising sun.

This expression, "The chief Musician," surely ought to come home to our hearts. Who is the chief Musician? We read, "In the midst of the congregation will I praise Thee" (Psa. 22:22), and the speaker is the Lord Jesus Christ Himself. It ought to give character to our songs of praise to realize that it is He who leads the praises of His people, and surely our songs of praise then should be, in some measure at least, worthy of Him. I am afraid sometimes we sing what we call gospel songs that He would never lead. But when we approach Him with reverence and in gratitude the Lord Jesus delights to lead out our praises. So when we see these Psalms dedicated "To the chief Musician" let us always think of Christ and say, "Here is something that the Spirit of God inspired David to write, and he dedicated it to the Lord Jesus Christ Himself."

It is an interesting fact that very frequently in the bool of Psalms the last verse of one Psalm is a key to the next one. We see that right here. The last verse of Psalm 19 ends up with the words, "O Lord, my strength, and my redeemer," and the 20th Psalm celebrates the strength and the redemption of our God. Then in the same way the last verse of the 20th Psalm says, "Save, Lord: let the King hear us when we call." And the 21st Psalm is the Psalm of the King in His glory. It begins, "The king shall joy in Thy strength, O Lord." When reading in the Psalms watch for those intimate connections. Sometimes you will get a series of five, six, seven, or nine Psalms all linked like that, the last verse of one introducing the first of the next with certain words, certain expressions common to each and seemingly binding these Psalms together like a golden chain. In Psalm 19 we have had the testimony of creation and the testimony of the Word of God, all telling of a Redeemer that God has provided. Then in Psalm 20 we have the redemption, the salvation which that Redeemer has obtained for us.

Look at the first three verses of Psalm 20. The soul is resting, as it were, upon the work that the Lord Jesus Christ has accomplished. "The Lord hear thee in the day of trouble; the name of the God of Jacob defend thee; Send thee help from the sanctuary, and strengthen thee out of Zion; Remember all thy offerings, and accept thy burnt sacrifice." Of course all the offerings and all the burnt sacrifices speak of Christ so everything here is based upon sacrifice. All future blessing for Israel and for the nations as well as for the individual soul rests upon the one offering of the Lord Jesus Christ on Calvary. All these sacrifices that were offered in the past dispensations were just so many pictures of the work that He accomplished there and it is on the basis of this that all blessing comes to us. It is because of His offering that God hears those who call. The God of Jacob will undertake for us.

I do love that term, "The God of Jacob." Do you know that only once in the Bible we read of "The God of Isaac" and only twice of "The God of Abraham"? Once we read of "The Lord God of Elijah" but about twenty-two times in the book of the Psalms we read of "The God of Jacob." Why does He call himself "The God of Jacob"? I think there are a number of suggestive thoughts. Perhaps the first is that He is the God that the poor sinner needs, for Jacob was a poor crooked stick from the time he first came into this world right on through the years. The name means "the grafter" or "the cheat," literally, "the heel catcher." A man who would trip another by catching his heel. It is like the flesh in every one of us; what heel catchers we are! But God is "The God of Jacob." Isaac was a nice, colorless sort of man. He never did anything exciting. He was never excitingly good, never excitingly bad. You might have thought that God would far rather have delighted to call Himself, "The God of Isaac," but only once in the Word is He so called. It is "The God of Jacob" because He wants you and me to know that He is the God who is interested in poor sinners. And then again I think the thought of "The God of Jacob" suggests the God of the individual. God singles people out. "I am that man's God," and He singled you and me out, and we can look up into His face and say, "Thou art my God." And then there is this thought, He is the God of patience, and what patience He had with Jacob! He dealt with him; He disciplined him; He took that crooked man and chastened, educated him, and taught him by discipline until at last when an old man he became a quiet, patient, godly worshiper. We read that Jacob, when he was dying, "worshipped, leaning upon the top of his staff" (Heb. 11:21). It took him a long time to reach that place but he attained it at last What patience God has had with some of us!

The last section includes verses 4 to 6 where we have the blessing that comes to the people of God in answer to prayer. Verses 1, 2, and 3 are in the nature of a prayer, and you notice they conclude with the word, "Selah." In our version the sentence is not completed but actually you should have a period there, for the word "Selah" itself would indicate that. This word "Selah" literally means "to lift up." Just as, for instance, in playing the piano the pianist comes to a rest and just lifts her hands for a moment. When the music was played the musician would just lift his hand and indicate that there was a rest in the music. When I was a boy, a dear old saint said, "Whenever I see that word 'Selah' I always read it as, 'Stop and consider!' " It is the Lord saying, "I have been telling you something of importance; you just stop now and think it over." It is divine punctuation. Stop and think this over before you go on with the next strain.

The fourth verse, instead of being a part of the petition, should be a declarative sentence. A better translation is this, "He will grant thee according to thine own heart, and fulfil all thy counsel." The prayer was in the other three verses, "May the Lord do thus and so for you," and now the answer comes, "He will grant thee according to thine own heart, and fulfil all thy counsel." Some one says, "Doesn't God always do that? does He not grant everybody according to his heart and fulfil all their counsels?" He has never promised to do that in an indiscriminate kind of way. But He does say, "Delight thyself also in the Lord; and He shall give thee the desires of thine heart" (Psa. 37:4). And again, "If ye abide in Me, and My words abide in you, ye shall ask what ye will, and it shall be done unto you" (John 15:7). Here, you see, you have the soul occupied with Christ, occupied with His work, and now the cry goes out to God on the cloud of the burnt sacrifices and the answer comes, "He will grant thee according to thine own heart, and fulfil all thy counsel." When you and I are really taken up with Him, when His will is our will, when we are delighting ourselves in Him, when His Word abides in us and we are consciously in communion with Him, we may ask what we will and it will be done. "Well," somebody said to me one time, "if that is true, why don't you ask the Lord for a million dollars and pay up everything and not have to take up any more collections?" I could not do that if I am delighting myself in Him. He does not tell me to ask for a million dollars. If He did, I would do it. When George Mueller delighted himself in Him and he asked for a million pounds, God gave it to him during a lifetime of fifty years, when running that orphanage. If I had a responsibility like that I could go to the Lord about it too. If you and I are really living in communion with Him the Holy Spirit dwelling within us will move our hearts and show us that for which we should ask, and as we pray in the Holy Spirit we can be assured of an answer.

Now then faith speaks in verses 5 and 6, "We will rejoice in Thy salvation, and in the name of our God we will set up our banners: the Lord fulfil all thy petitions." In verse 6 you have a term used that refers throughout all the prophetic Scripture to our Lord Jesus Himself, that which the Jews used for the coming Saviour, "Now know I that the Lord saveth His anointed." "Anointed" is the same as "Messiah." The Messiah was the One for whom the Jews were waiting all down through the centuries. But it was predicted that God's Anointed was to suffer, to be rejected, to die, and then was to come forth from the grave in triumph. And so the Psalmist looks on to the day of victory and says, "Now know I that the Lord saveth His anointed; He will hear him from His holy heaven with the saving strength of His right hand." And the same power that raised Messiah from the dead is the power that undertakes for us. So we can say, "Some trust in chariots, and some in horses: but we will remember the name of the Lord our God." We are trusting in God alone. How apt we are in the hour of stress and trial to turn for help to that which is merely earthly or human and so often fails us. If you once know the blessedness of depending on God, you will find it is a luxury to trust in Him. Your confidence will not be in the natural but in the spiritual.

They are brought down"—those who trust only in temporal things—"and fallen: but we"—we who trust in God—"are risen, and stand upright" The Psalm closes with Christ in view. "Save, Lord: let the King hear us when we call." And of course the King is none other than our blessed Lord Jesus. And that introduces us directly to Psalm 21, for the very first verse, as we have seen, celebrates the glory of the King.

"The king shall joy in Thy strength, O Lord; and in Thy salvation how greatly shall he rejoice." In other Psalms we have seen the blessed Lord walking through this earth in lowly subjection to the Father. Now we see Him, the risen One, ready to take His great power and reign as He will in God's appointed time, rejoicing in the deliverance that came when God raised Him up from the dead. And the Psalmist says, "Thou hast given Him His heart's desire, and hast not withholden the request of His lips." What was the heart's desire of the Lord Jesus? What was it that took Him to that cross, that took Him through Gethsemane, that sustained Him in those hours of darkness? The Apostle Paul tells us. He says, "Who for the joy that was set before Him endured the cross, despising the shame" (Heb. 12:2). What was that joy? It was the joy of having you and me together with Him in the glory. What an amazing thing—His heart's desire was to have us with Him in heaven! That is what Isaiah means when he pictures the awful agony of the Cross and then says, "He shall see of the travail of His soul, and shall be satisfied" (Isa. 53:11). The word "travail" refers only to one kind of suffering, and that is to the pangs of birth. And so Isaiah says, His awful agony on the Cross was the means of giving us life, of bringing salvation to us. "He shall see of the travail of His soul, and shall be satisfied." "Thou hast given Him His heart's desire." He is now at God's right hand in the glory, and there will be millions through eternity who will owe everything to His precious blood. That will be the fulfillment of His heart's desire. The Psalmist has rather in view the kingdom on earth, but we may think of both.

"Thou preventest Him with the blessings of goodness: Thou settest a crown of pure gold on His head." We sing, "Crown Him," but the fact of the matter is, we are not going to crown Him. Of course what is meant is that we will participate in His coronation, but it is God the Father who crowns Him. Men crowned Him once. They put upon Him the fruit of the earth that was cursed. God said to the earth, when Adam had sinned, "Thorns and thistles shall it bring forth" (Gen. 3:18), and they put a crown of thorns on the head of my Saviour. But God has torn away the crown of thorns, and we read, "Thou settest a crown of pure gold on His head. He asked life of Thee, and Thou gavest it Him, even length of days for ever and ever." He was going to death but counted on God the Father to raise Him and to give Him "length of days for ever and ever," and so we have resurrection blessing for all who trust Him.

"His glory is great in Thy salvation: honour and majesty hast Thou laid upon Him. For Thou hast made Him most blessed for ever: Thou hast made Him exceeding glad with Thy countenance. For the king trusteth in the Lord, and through the mercy of the most High He shall not be moved." See how the humanity of our Lord again shines forth. He came into this scene as Man; He went to the Cross as Man; as Man He committed His soul to the Father, "Father, into Thy hands I commend My spirit" (Luke 23:46); as man He went down into death, but now God the Father has raised Him from the dead, and He is come forth in resurrection glory in a life that can never again be destroyed, that can never come to an end, life for ever and ever. And now until that glad day when He yields up the kingdom to the Father He is still the subject One, He is still serving the Father as He is seeking to bring men to Himself and preparing the way for His coming glorious kingdom. When at last everything has been subdued to God He will deliver up the kingdom to the Father.

In verses 8 to the end of this Psalm we have Messiah reigning and the effect of that reign upon man here on earth. When He descends in power and glory to take the kingdom He is going to root out, we are told, all things that offend, and so we read, "Thine hand shall find out all Thine enemies: Thy right hand shall find out those that hate Thee." What a sad thing to think that after all the infinite love and grace that God has shown to the world through the Lord Jesus Christ there are still myriads of men who hate Him, who have no desire to be reconciled to Him. And when He comes again in power and glory He is going to destroy the wicked out of the earth, that a kingdom of righteousness may be set up in this very scene. "Thou shalt make them as a fiery oven in the time of Thine anger: the Lord shall swallow them up in His wrath, and the fire shall devour them." Now turn to a New Testament passage that touches on exactly this same thing. The Second Epistle to the Thessalonians, chapter 1, verses 6–10, "Seeing it is a righteous thing with God to recompense tribulation to them that trouble you; And to you who are troubled rest." When God recompenses tribulation to His enemies He will give rest to His own. "To you who are troubled rest with us, when the Lord Jesus shall be revealed from heaven with His mighty angels, In flaming fire taking vengeance on them that know not God, and that obey not the gospel of our Lord Jesus Christ: Who shall be punished with everlasting destruction from the presence of the Lord, and from the glory of His power; When He shall come to be glorified in His saints, and to be admired in all them that believe (because our testimony among you was believed) in that day." This is the day when the kingdom is to be introduced, and it begins with the Lord taking vengeance on His enemies.

In the third chapter of Malachi's prophecy we read of a group in the last days to whom the things of God are precious; and when Israel will be going through the time of Jacob's trouble this little group will come together to search His Word and to wait upon Him, and He says of them, in verse 17, "And they shall be Mine, saith the Lord of hosts, in that day when I make up My jewels; and I will spare them, as a man spareth his own son that serveth him." Spare them from what? from the judgment that is coming upon men. "Then shall ye return, and discern between the righteous and the wicked, between him that serveth God and him that serveth Him not" (verse 18). Now in chapter 4 we read, "For, behold, the day cometh, that shall burn as an oven; and all the proud, yea, and all that do wickedly, shall be stubble: and the day that cometh shall burn them up, saith the Lord of hosts, that it shall leave them neither root nor branch." What a complete destruction of all the wicked in that day, the day of Jehovah's power. But now see the blessings for the righteous. It is of people who will be living then on this earth that He speaks. "But unto you that fear My name [and He is speaking to men of Israel] shall the Sun of righteousness arise with healing in His wings; and ye shall go forth, and grow up as calves of the stall. And ye shall tread down the wicked; for they shall be ashes under the soles of your feet in the day that I shall do this, saith the Lord of hosts." I have often had some of these materialists come to me and point to a scripture like this and say, "You tell us that the Bible teaches the eternal conscious punishment of those who reject the Lord Jesus Christ"

And I say, "Yes, terrible as it is I find it in my Book, and I dare not teach men anything else."

"But look," they say, "in this passage it says that in the day of judgment the Lord is going to consume them root and branch and they will be ashes. Well, then, there won't be anything left."

But he is not speaking here of the final day of judgment, the great white throne, he is speaking of a judgment that is going to take place on this earth when King Messiah returns to reign, and the wicked on the earth shall be destroyed with the brightness of His presence, burning up root and branch, that is, father and son, and the righteous will be spared to enter into the millennial kingdom and all that will be left will be ashes. That has to do only with the body. You cannot burn a soul or a spirit to ashes. Suppose that you had been there the day after Sodom and Gomorrah were destroyed, when fire had come down and burned up those cities. Suppose Abraham had gone down there, he could have walked the streets of Sodom and Gomorrah, and the wicked, the bodies of the wicked, would have been ashes under his feet. This has nothing to do with their souls. It is a judgment here on this earth. Look at those people who died so long ago. Are they annihilated? What does Jesus say? He says, speaking of the cities where most of His mighty works had been done, "I say unto you, It shall be more tolerable for Tyre and Sidon at the day of judgment, than for you." "For if the mighty works, which were done in you, had been done in Tyre and Sidon, they would have repented long ago in sackcloth and ashes" (Matt. 11:22, 21). They were ashes under the feet of the righteous, but they are coming up in the day of judgment. Their spirits, their souls were not ashes and even their bodies are going to be raised from the dead, and they will stand in the day of judgment. And so this judgment is that which takes place on the earth when the Lord Jesus will be revealed "In flaming fire taking vengeance on them that know not God."

"Thou shalt make them as a fiery oven in the time of Thine anger: the Lord shall swallow them up in His wrath, and the fire shall devour them. Their fruit shalt Thou destroy from the earth, and their seed from among the children of men." The generation of the wicked is blotted out in order that righteousness may reign for a thousand wonderful years. "For they intended evil against Thee: they imagined a mischievous device, which they are not able to perform. Therefore shalt Thou make them turn their back, when Thou shalt make ready Thine arrows upon Thy strings against the face of them." The Lord is represented here as coming from heaven with a mighty army and like a bowman putting His arrow to the bow and His enemies fleeing before Him when He descends to deal with them in judgment.

The Psalm closes with an ascription of praise, "Be Thou exalted, Lord, in Thine own strength; so will we sing and praise Thy power." Oh, what a day it will be when wickedness will no longer be permitted to have the ascendency.

THE SHEPHERD PSALMS
PSALMS 22, 23, AND 24

IT HAS BEEN POINTED OUT OFTEN THAT OUR BLESSED LORD is referred to in the New Testament as the Shepherd under three different aspects. In John 10 He says, "I am the good Shepherd." In Hebrews 13 He is called "the great Shepherd" as "brought again from the dead," and in 1 Peter 5, looking on to His second coming when the under shepherds will give an account to Him, He is spoken of as "the chief Shepherd." Some one long ago suggested that in Psalm 22 we have the Good Shepherd giving His life for the sheep; in Psalm 23, the Chief Shepherd in resurrection life guiding His people through the wilderness of this world, and in Psalm 24, the Great Shepherd coming again in power and glory to bring in everlasting blessing.

In the early part of the book of Leviticus we have five different offerings. Four of these involved the sacrifice of life; the other one did not. The one in which there was no sacrifice of life is called the meal or the meat offering, the word "meat" being used there for food, the food offering. We have seen already that in Psalm 16 we have the blessed Lord Jesus presented as the meal offering, and this speaks of the perfection of His life. Every act of that holy life of His went up to God as something in which He could delight. The other offerings are the burnt offering, the peace offering, the sin offering, and the trespass offering. Psalm 40 is the Psalm of the burnt offering, Psalm 85 is that of the peace offering, Psalm 69 that of the trespass offering, and Psalm 22 is the Psalm of the sin offering.

In the sin offering we have the Lord Jesus Christ made sin for us "that we might be made the righteousness of God in Him." The New Testament does not tell us a great deal of what went on in the heart and mind of our blessed Lord when He was undergoing the awful judgment of God against sin, but we have something that guides us and helps us to understand in the fact that just as the three hours of darkness were coming to an end the Lord Jesus cried in the agony of His soul, "My God, My God, why hast Thou forsaken Me?" (Matt. 27:46). That immediately carries our minds back to this 22d Psalm. It tells us that it is a Messianic Psalm; and when we turn to consider it, we find that it gives us the thoughts of the heart of our blessed Lord during those hours of darkness when He was taking our place, when He was made sin for us.

This Psalm begins with what someone has called "Immanuel's orphaned cry," "My God, My God, why hast Thou forsaken Me?" And in the Hebrew text it ends with His cry of triumph, "It is finished!" You will not find this in our authorized version but will find the words, "They shall come, and shall declare His righteousness unto a people that shall be born, that He hath done *this*." You will observe that the word "this" is in italics which means that there is nothing in the original text answering to it. It is supplied by the editor. In the Hebrew the neuter and the masculine pronouns are exactly the same, and this is in the middle voice so that actually it could be translated, "They shall come, and shall declare His righteousness unto a people that shall be born, that it is finished." So it begins with the cry that speaks of Him as the great sin offering, and it ends with the cry that tells that His work is finished.

The Psalm divides into two parts, the first twenty-one verses stand together, and then from verses 22 to 31 we have the second division. In the first twenty-one verses the holy Sufferer is alone—

> "Alone He bare the cross,
> Alone its grief sustained."

There is no one associated with Him. There are enemies reproaching Him, but He is alone as He bears our sins before God. But in the last part, from verse 22 on, He has brethren who are associated with Him, and so in verse 22 we enter into His resurrection life, the work of the Cross all in the past.

Think of Him hanging there. And may I again remind you that before He entered into these experiences He had already been three hours upon the Cross. The Lord Jesus was nailed to the Cross at about 9 o'clock in the morning. He was taken down a little after 3 o'clock in the afternoon. From 9 o'clock until noon He was suffering at the hands of man, the sun was shining down upon the scene, and man was visiting upon Him every fiendish agony that a wicked heart, energized by Satan, could devise. But in those three hours you do not find the blessed Lord uttering one word that indicated the least self-pity, that would even suggest that He has any concern for Himself. In those three hours He prays; He speaks but always has others in view; He looks down at the foot of the Cross and sees His blessed mother, Mary, and John standing near, and He says to John, "Behold thy mother," and to Mary, "Behold thy son." And John led her away from the scene of the Saviour's dying agony. Then He looks at the multitude all about Him, their mouths filled with blasphemy and their minds with hatred, and looks heavenward and cries, "Father, forgive them; for they know not what they do" (Luke 23:34). He opens the door of a city of refuge for them that they may enter in as having slain a man without knowing what they were doing, so that there may be forgiveness. Then He turns to the thief hanging by His side, who has recognized in that thorn-crowned man Israel's true Messiah and who owned his own sin and cried, "Lord remember me when Thou comest into Thy kingdom" (Luke 23:42). And the Saviour said, as it were, "You won't have to wait until I come into My kingdom—today shalt thou be with Me in paradise." And he was, for that day ended at 6 o'clock at night, at sunset, but before 6 o'clock the Saviour had died and the thief had died and the two were together in paradise.

At high noon the sun is blotted out from the heaven: darkness spreads over all the scene, darkness so dense that one cannot see another—and that was a picture, a symbol of the deeper darkness that had wrapped the soul of the Son of God. Now God began to deal with Him about our sins. Remember, it was not the physical suffering of Jesus that put away sin; it was what He endured in His innermost Being. Isaiah says, "When Thou shalt make His *soul* an offering for sin" (Isa. 53:10). What He suffered from the hands of man could not atone for sin, but what He suffered from the hands of God during those three hours of darkness settled the sin question. All that our sins deserved fell on the sacred Son of God, and He was absolutely silent, like a lamb dumb before her shearers, until just as the three hours were coming to an end, it seemed as though His great heart burst with the agony of it all; and then came the cry with which this Psalm begins, "My God, My God, why hast Thou forsaken Me?" Do you know the answer to that question? Well, I am the answer to it and so are you. Why was He forsaken? In order that I might not be forsaken. In order that you might not be forsaken. It was because He was bearing our sins, taking our place, because He was made sin for us.

Listen to His cry now, and understand, these are the thoughts of His heart He is looking up to God in those hours of darkness, and He says, "Why art Thou so far from helping me, and from the words of my roaring? O my God, I cry in the daytime, but Thou hearest not; and in the night season, and am not silent" But there is no complaint, He accepts it all from God and says, "But Thou art holy, O Thou that inhabitest the praises of Israel." And it was because of the holiness of God that He could not interfere to spare His own Son. When He was taking the sinner's place, judgment had to fall on Him.

Listen to Him again as He addresses God, He looked back over all the history of the chosen people and said, "Our fathers trusted in Thee: they trusted, and Thou didst deliver them. They cried unto Thee, and were delivered: they trusted in Thee, and were not confounded. But I am a worm, and no man; a reproach of men, and despised of the people." Here He, the holy One, is in contrast to every good man in all past ages. It was never known that God forsook a righteous man. There He is on that Cross, the absolutely righteous One, dying, forsaken of God. Oh, He says, I have gone down lower than any man ever went before, "I am a worm, and no man." The word He used for worm is the word "tola," and the tola of the orient is a little worm something like the cochineal of Mexico which feeds on a certain kind of cactus. The people beat these plants until the cochineal fall into a basin and then they crush those little insects and the blood is that brilliant crimson dye that makes those bright Mexican garments. In Palestine and Syria they use the tola in the same way and it makes the beautiful permanent scarlet dye of the orient It was very expensive and was worn only by the great and the rich and the noble. It is referred to again and again in Scripture. Solomon is said to have clothed the maidens of Israel in scarlet. Daniel was to be clothed in scarlet by Belshazzar. And that word "scarlet" is literally "the splendor of a worm." "They shall be clothed in the splendor of a worm." Now the Lord Jesus Christ says, "I am a worm; I am the tola," and He had to be crushed in death that you and I might be clothed in glory. The glorious garments of our salvation are the garments that have been procured as a result of His death and His suffering. What a wicked thing to refuse the garment of salvation, to think of spurning it and turning away from it when Christ had to go through so much in order to prepare it for us.

Imagine the effrontery of the man who went into the marriage-feast without having a wedding garment when the king had provided one for him. He spurned the king's bounty. When the king exclaimed, "Friend, how camest thou in hither not having a Wedding garment?" (Matt. 22:12) he was speechless. If you are unsaved, what will you say when you stand before God in the day of doom and He says, "Friend, what are you doing here without the garment of salvation that was purchased for you by the death of My Son? Why do you not have that garment of salvation? Why are you not dressed in that robe of righteousness?" What can you say when it was offered you so freely, when you might have had it? I think the most awful thought that will ever come to a lost soul in the pit of woe is this, "Jesus died; yet I am in hell. He died to purchase salvation for me, and fool that I am I spurned it and I am lost forever." Can you imagine anything worse than that? Think of the grace of our Lord Jesus, who "though He was rich, yet for your sakes He became poor, that ye through His poverty might be rich" (2 Cor. 8:9). He became the tola, crushed in death that we might be robed in glory.

And then as He hangs on the Cross He can hear the muttering of the crowd in the dark, and He says, "All they that see Me laugh Me to scorn: they shoot out the lip, they shake the head, saying, He trusted on the Lord that He would deliver Him: let Him deliver Him, seeing He delighted in Him. But Thou art He that took Me out of the womb: Thou didst make Me hope when I was upon My mother's breasts. I was cast upon Thee from the womb; Thou art My God from the body of My mother's belly." Do you see what is involved in this remarkable scripture? Even as that little Babe came into the world He had full consciousness of His relationship to the Father. But He was both God and Man in one Person. And now He cries, "Be not far from Me; for trouble is near; for there is none to help." Then He sees the leaders in Israel gathered against Him and says, "Many bulls have compassed Me: strong bulls of Bashan have beset Me round. They gaped upon Me with their mouths, as a ravening and a roaring lion." See the bulls of Bashan. They were clean beasts that could be offered in sacrifice and are used here to signify the great and mighty leaders in Israel who should have been His friends, but they are there arrayed against Him.

And now note the description of Him hanging upon the Cross, "I am poured out like water, and all My bones are out of joint." As He hangs there upon the Cross it seems as though every joint will be torn asunder. "My heart is like wax; it is melted in the midst of My bowels. My strength is dried up like a potsherd." Think of His thirst as i He hung there during all the morning of that hot spring day. He cries, "My tongue cleaveth to My jaws; and Thou hast brought Me into the dust of death." And then He looks at the Gentiles round about joining with the Jews, and He says, "For dogs have compassed Me." Dogs are the unclean Gentiles. "The assembly of the wicked have inclosed Me: they pierced My hands and My feet" What a perfect description! And it was written a thousand years before Jesus died, and it is all fulfilled as He hangs upon that Cross for you and for me.

He who was so pure, He who was so perfectly holy, He whose mind never had an evil or an unclean thought, hung there before that assembled crowd practically naked, put to shame before them all, and He says, "I may tell all My bones: they look and stare upon Me." At the foot of the Cross the soldiers, calloused, hard, indifferent, parted His garments. "They part My garments among them, and cast lots upon My vesture." They gamble for His clothes as the Son of God hangs naked on the Cross, put to shame for sinners.

But He looks to the Father, as Satan now comes against Him, "But be not Thou far from Me, O Lord: O My strength, haste Thee to help Me. Deliver My soul from the sword; My darling" (my only one)—it is His own soul He is speaking of here—"from the power of the dog"—the dog of the pit is Satan. "Save me from the lion's mouth." It is the lion of hell, Satan waiting and saying, "Now in a moment I will have His soul; I will have Him where I want Him, and He will never come out of death again." "Save Me from the lion's mouth." Then the next moment all the suffering is over; the darkness is gone. In the New Testament we hear Him say, "Father, into Thy hands I commend My spirit" (Luke 23:46).

"Thou hast heard Me from the horns of the unicorns." There is no such thing as a unicorn. Our translators put that word in because they did not understand the exact meaning, but every Hebrew scholar now knows that it is the aurochs, a wild ox with great branching horns, as sharp almost as needles at the ends. The executioners used to lay hold of poor, wretched, condemned victims, bind them by the feet and the shoulders upon those sharp horns and then set the wild ox loose in the desert to run about until the man died. That is the picture that is used here. Crucifixion was like putting one upon the horns of the wild ox. "Thou hast heard Me from the horns of the unicorns."

The suffering is over now, the darkness disappears. He commits His spirit to the Father, and then we pass into the next verse, and He who was alone is no longer alone. He who bore the Cross alone now has company. Who are His companions? those who owe everything for eternity to the work He did upon that Cross. This is Jesus in resurrection now. "I will declare Thy name unto My brethren: in the midst of the congregation will I praise Thee." In the Epistle to the Hebrews it is translated, "In the midst of the church will I sing praise unto Thee." Here is the blessed Lord brought up from death and now He takes His place in the midst of the company of the redeemed and leads out their hearts in praise. Here is the Chief Musician.

> "Join the singing that He leadeth,
> Now to God your voices raise,
> Every path that we have trodden

Is a triumph of His grace."

He is going to lead the singing forever. He will lead out our hearts in praise to God for all eternity.

Then the Spirit of Christ, speaking through the Psalmist, turns to Israel, "Ye that fear the Lord, praise Him; all ye the seed of Jacob, glorify Him; and fear Him, all ye the seed of Israel. For He hath not despised nor abhorred the affliction of the afflicted one." It is the singular there. While God as Judge had to turn away His face yet God as Father never forsook Jesus. He was never dearer to the heart of the Father than at the time that the Judge could not interfere.

Suppose such a case as a young man very much loved of his father committing some grievous crime and brought into court, and when he comes into the court room, sitting on the judge's bench is his own father. The evidence is brought in, the young man is proven guilty, and that judge has to pronounce sentence on him.

The son says, "Father, Father, you are surely not going to do that to me!"

"Young man, in this room I am dealing with you, not as your father but as your judge."

And yet his father's heart may be breaking over the plight in which his son is found. And so God as Judge had to deal with His Son about our sins at the very moment that God as Father was yearning over Jesus, and how gladly He received Him when He came forth in triumph from the tomb! And so He says, "My praise shall be of Thee in the great congregation: I will pay My vows before them that fear Him. The meek shall eat and be satisfied." Because of the great banquet that love has spread those lowly enough to come as confessed sinners may be satisfied. "They shall praise the Lord that seek Him: your heart shall live for ever." And see the wide extent of the benefits of His work, "All the ends of the world shall remember and turn unto the Lord: and all the kindreds of the nations shall worship before Thee." This has not been fulfilled yet, but it will be when the Lord shall come in power and great glory. "For the kingdom is the Lord's: and He is the governor among the nations. All they that be fat upon earth shall eat and worship: all they that go down to the dust shall bow before Him: even Him who did not keep alive His own soul." That is Dr. Young's striking translation. The whole world bowing down before that blessed Man who did not keep alive His own soul but went into death for us.

But in the meantime while waiting for the full day of the King, "A seed shall serve Him; it shall be accounted to the Lord for a generation. They shall come, and shall declare His righteousness unto a people that shall be born, that it is finished."

> *"It is finished, yes indeed,*
> *Finished every jot.*
> *Sinner, this is all you need,*
> *Tell me, is it not?"*

It is the Good Shepherd now. Have you trusted the Good Shepherd? Well, where is He now? He is not on the Cross any more. God has raised Him from the dead and taken Him to highest glory, and He is there as the Great Shepherd guiding His people through the world, providing for their need.

Psalm 23

I do not need to comment very much on Psalm 23. Some one has said, "I believe Psalm 23 is the most loved Psalm of them all, and it is the one least believed." Do you believe it? You love it, do you not? And you like to say, "The Lord is my Shepherd; I shall not want" But the next time that you are thrown out of a job are you going to say, "Oh dear, I don't know what on earth I am going to do"? What was that about the Shepherd? "The Lord is my Shepherd; I shall not want." And when sickness and bereavement come, do you say, "Oh my, it is all up with me"? Is He no longer your Shepherd? Do you say these words over and yet not believe them? "The Lord is my Shepherd; I shall not want." I like the way the little girl put it when she got up to recite in Sunday school. She said, "The Lord is my Shepherd; I should worry," and ran down to her seat. She meant, I shouldn't worry. Oh yes, He who died for me lives for me and has promised to undertake.

"The Lord is my Shepherd; I shall not want." I shall not want rest for, "He maketh me to lie down in green pastures." You would think that people would have sense enough to lie down when tired. The trouble with a lot of people is that they keep running until they have nervous breakdowns, Jesus says, "Come ye yourselves apart into a desert place, and rest a while" (Mark 6:31). I shall not want refreshment for "He leadeth me beside the still waters." I shall not want restoration, "He restoreth my soul." I shall not want guidance for "He leadeth me in the paths of righteousness for His name's sake." I shall not want companionship in the hour of trial, in the time when the dark, dark shadows of death fall athwart my path for, "Yea, though I walk through the valley of the shadow of death, I will fear no evil: for Thou art with me." I shall not want comfort for "Thy rod and Thy staff they comfort me." I shall not want provision, "Thou preparest a table before me in the presence of mine enemies." I shall not want unction for "Thou anointest my head with oil." I shall not want satisfaction, "My cup runneth over." I shall not want goodness or mercy for "Surely goodness and mercy shall follow me all the days of my life." And I shall not want a home at last for "I will dwell in the house of the Lord for ever." Do you believe it? Then do not ever go around with your head hanging down any more. If all these things are true, why should our hearts be bowed down like a bulrush? The Great Shepherd has undertaken to see us through.

Psalm 24

Now Psalm 24 carries us on to the day of the kingdom, that kingdom intimated in verse 28 of Psalm 22. The day of the kingdom is the day of the Lord's return and it is when He comes again that He comes as the Chief Shepherd, and so now you have a description of this world when Jesus comes to reign. "The earth is the Lord's, and the fulness thereof; the world, and they that dwell therein. For He hath founded it upon the seas, and established it upon the floods." Who has title to it? "Who shall ascend into the hill of the Lord? or who shall stand in His holy place?" There is only One. Whatever title you and I have we get in association with Him, for there is only One to whom these words fully apply. "He that hath clean hands." The hands of Jesus were never stained with sin. "And a pure heart." The heart of Jesus was never unclean. "Who hath not lifted up His soul unto vanity." The soul of Jesus was never proud. "Nor sworn deceitfully." There was no guile found in His mouth.

"He shall receive the blessing from the Lord, and righteousness from the God of His salvation." And He receives it for us, and we are made "accepted in the Beloved." "This is the generation of them that seek Him, that seek Thy face, O Jacob." For in the day of the kingdom of Israel, Jacob will be restored to the Lord and will become a means of blessing to the whole world. And now we have the antiphonal song that we have often heard. The King is coming; see, He is entering in to take possession of His royal palace, and as His outriders lead the way and draw near the royal palace, they shout aloud, "Lift up your heads, O ye gates; and be ye lift up, ye everlasting doors [really, doors of eternity]; and the King of glory shall come in." And from within there comes the cry, "Who is this King of glory?" And the retainers of the King cry, "The Lord strong and mighty, the Lord mighty in battle," for the Son of Man is Jehovah incarnate. "Lift up your heads, O ye gates; even lift them up, ye everlasting doors [doors of eternity]; and the King of glory shall come in." And again from within comes the inquiry, "Who is this King of glory?" And the answer, "The Lord of hosts, He is the King of glory." And Jesus takes the kingdom; the Crucified sits on the throne of David and reigns in power and glory. What a wonderful trilogy we have here in these three Psalms. The Psalm of the Cross, 22; the Psalm of the crook, the Shepherd's crook, 23; the Psalm of the crown, 24. And they tell the whole wonderful story of His humiliation and His glory.

THE BASIS OF CONFIDENCE
PSALMS 25, 26, AND 27

WE HAVE BEEN NOTICING IN STUDYING THIS BOOK HOW very frequently a number of Psalms are intimately linked together. Beginning with Psalm 25 and going on through Psalm 39 we have a little group of fifteen Psalms all of which deal with the same general subject, that is, the spiritual exercises of the people of God, particularly the coming remnant of Israel in the days of the great tribulation, but also the exercises that the people of God in general, pass through in this world while waiting for the coming again of our Lord Jesus Christ.

Of course we need to remember in studying the Psalms that we are not actually on Christian ground. The disciples of our blessed Lord were never definitely known as Christians until the present glorious dispensation of the grace of God came to us. Of old they were children of God but waiting for the full knowledge of redemption. They had real faith, and so they were born again; but they did not know what we know, an accomplished redemption and the veil rent so that believers may go right into the presence of God. By and by, after the Church of God has been taken out of this scene, there will be what Scripture calls "the tribulation," when our Lord turns again to Israel to take out a remnant from among them, to open their eyes and to prepare them for the coming of the King, when He begins His glorious reign. During that time they will be in great measure in the same state of soul as believers were of old before the Cross, because, while they will have learned from the study of the Scriptures that Jesus, the Jesus whom their fathers rejected, was really Messiah, it will not be until He actually appears that they will enter into the full knowledge of redemption. And so we do not find that their worship rises to the full height of Christian worship. There is always with them a certain measure of uncertainty of things. They do not have the clear, definite knowledge of justification from all things that is given to the Church of God today. They are groping largely, and yet their hearts are yearning after God.

When we come to consider these fifteen Psalms we find that they all have to do with the exercises of God's people; and yet they fall into three groups. The first five of them, Psalms 25 to 29, deal largely with the basis or the ground of the souls' confidence as they look up to God because they are conscious of His abiding love and of the integrity of their own hearts. That is, they know that they are seeking to do the will of God. Then in the second section, Psalms 30 to 34, we seem to move on a step and find these Psalms occupied with the hearts' appropriation of God's salvation. They seem to have risen largely above themselves and the question of their own personal integrity to realize that salvation rests entirely upon the matchless grace of God. And then in the third section, Psalms 35 to 39, they are occupied largely with the question of personal holiness. They are brought consciously into the presence of God, and as they realize His infinite holiness there is on their part a yearning desire to be more and more like Him. So we can see that believers who used the book of Psalms in the old days before the veil was rent and believers who will use the book in the coming day of the great tribulation have not the same light that we have today. Yet the moral order is the same. When we first come to Christ, if we come to Him sincerely and seek honestly to walk with Him, the moment the soul becomes conscious of failure, of sin, there is a cloud on the sense of assurance. As we go on and learn to turn from self altogether and to be occupied with Christ and His finished work, and as we progress in the Christian life we are occupied not so much with the question of the putting away of our sin and our final salvation, but, as a sense of His infinite holiness becomes more real to us, we find our hearts crying out for holiness of heart and cleanness of life.

Look then at Psalm 25. Here we find a sense of God's righteousness and grace leading the heart out to Him. This is divided in a rather striking way. First, in verses 1 to 7 we have a prayer; in verses 8 to 10 we have the soul's recognition of God's goodness, and again in verse 11 there is a prayer. Then in verses 12 to 15 we get the soul's testimony, and verses 16 to 22 close the Psalm with another prayer. Look at the first prayer, "Unto thee, O Lord, do I lift up my soul. O my God, I trust in Thee: let me not be ashamed, let not mine enemies triumph over me. Yea, let none that wait on Thee be ashamed: let them be ashamed which transgress without cause." Somebody has very well said that David might have written this Psalm when he was fleeing from Absalom, when perfectly conscious of his own integrity of heart, though he could not forget the sins of years ago, and he was able to trust Him in spite of his difficult circumstances. You remember how beautifully that came out in his case when Shimei, the Benjamite, threw stones at David and cried, "Thou bloody man, and thou man of Belial" (2 Sam. 16:7), and Abishai, one of David's friends, said, "Why should this dead dog curse my lord the king? let me go over, I pray thee, and take off his head" (2 Sam. 16:9). But David said, "Let him curse; because the Lord hath said unto him, Curse David. Who shall then say, Wherefore hast thou done so? And David said to Abishai, and to all his servants, Behold, my son, which came forth of my bowels, seeketh my life: how much more now may this Benjamite do it? let him alone, and let him curse, for the Lord hath bidden him" (2 Sam. 16:10, 11). The Lord can turn the curse into a blessing. David realized deep in his heart that the suffering was to a certain extent the result of that sin of so long ago in the case of Bath-sheba. God was still visiting that sin upon him governmentally, but David could just accept it as from God, for he was conscious that he had judged his sin and was seeking to walk faithfully with the Lord, and so he could look up to God and plead, in that sense, his own integrity. If we think of David as in those circumstances when he wrote these words it may help us to understand them better. We cannot say positively that they were written at that time, but they would fit that occasion in a wonderful way.

"Shew me Thy ways, O Lord; teach me Thy paths. Lead me in Thy truth, and teach me: for Thou art the God of my salvation; on Thee do I wait all the day." How proper it is that such a prayer should be on our lips and in our hearts! We who have been redeemed to God, can we not take our place with David and pray the same words? Is not this what we want above everything else? But mark this, God will never answer this prayer unless we give much time to the reverent study of His Word. He is not going to teach us His paths; He is not going to make known His truth by some wonderful revelation to us. He has given us all that we need for guidance and direction here in the Book, and He commands us to "Search the Scriptures." Our Lord Jesus prayed, "Sanctify them through Thy truth, Thy word is truth." Is it not a lamentable fact that we let our Bibles lie unopened upon the desk or the shelf or table day by day and hardly ever look into them unless it be when we come to a service? We do so little real waiting on God over His Word and yet we cry, "Show me Thy ways, O Lord; teach me Thy paths." He will never teach us His ways, He will never show us His paths if we neglect our Bibles. It is as we study the Word that He makes known His truth.

Then the Psalmist looks over the past, and three times he uses the word, "remember." "*Remember*, O Lord, Thy tender mercies and Thy lovingkindnesses; for they have been ever of old." As much as to say, "Lord, I am in deep distress, but remember how Thou didst take me up in my great need, Thou didst not save me because of any goodness Thou sawest in me; Thou didst take me up in grace. Remember all Thy past dealings; now deal with me still in mercy." Then he thinks of failures, of sins committed long ago which he has confessed and judged but which often came to his mind in after years, and he says, "*Remember* not the sins of my youth, nor my transgressions: according to Thy mercy *remember* Thou me for Thy goodness' sake, O Lord."

About twenty years ago I was called to see an aged saint of about ninety years of age whom we had known as a very godly man. I went into the room where he lay upon his bed and started to speak to him of the goodness of the Lord through all the years, but he stopped me and said, "I wonder whether you can help me; everything seems so dark."

"Dark?" I said, "you have known the Lord for nearly seventy years, and you have been such a help and blessing to others."

"Yes, but in my illness, since I have been lying here so weak my memory keeps bringing up the sins of my youth, and I cannot get them out of my mind. They keep crowding in upon me, and I cannot help thinking of them; they make me so miserable and wretched."

I turned to this passage, "Remember not the sins of my youth, nor my transgressions: according to Thy mercy remember me for Thy goodness' sake, O Lord," and I pointed out to him that all those sins were long since put away. I said, "You came to God seventy years ago; you confessed the sins of your youth, did you not?"

"I am afraid," he said, "that I forgot some of them."

I said, "It is not a question of being able to remember every individual sin. You acknowledged that your life had been a life of sin, and do you not remember what happened then?" His mind was very weak, and I said, "Don't you remember that when you confessed your sins, God said, Their sins and iniquities will I remember no more'? If God has forgotten them, why should you think about them?"

He looked at me and smiled and said, "I am an old fool remembering what God has forgotten." So he rested on the word of the Lord and was at peace.

In verses 8 and 9 David gives his testimony, "Good and upright is the Lord: therefore will He teach sinners in the way. The meek will He guide in judgment: and the meek will He teach His way. All the paths of the Lord are mercy and truth unto such as keep His covenant and His testimonies." And he just rests upon the covenant of God. God has given His Word, and we can depend on it. We can count on it. But notice how he puts the emphasis on the right state of the soul if one would enjoy the favor of God, "The meek will He guide in judgment." Do you know why so many of us miss our way? It is because we are not meek enough to be guided. "Judgment" here means discernment. Do you know why so many of us blunder? It is because we are so self-sufficient. Meekness is not natural to the human heart It is a grace communicated to those who walk in fellowship with God. "Take My yoke upon you, and learn of Me; for I am meek and lowly in heart" (Matt. 11:29). In one of the Minor Prophets we read, "Seek righteousness [discernment], seek meekness" (Zeph. 2:3). If you want the mind of God, if you want to understand His will, there must be an end to self-sufficiency. God hates pride; He hates self-sufficiency. There must be a sense of brokenness and lowliness in order that we may hear His voice.

David offers a wonderful prayer in the next verse. "For Thy name's sake, O Lord, pardon mine iniquity; for it is great." You might have expected him to have put it in the opposite way and to have said, "O Lord, pardon mine iniquity, for it is not very great. I was really entrapped into this." A lot of people do that; they make excuses for their iniquity and hope in that way to escape the punishment due to sin, but when a man takes his place honestly before God and says, "I have no excuses to make; my iniquity is great," he finds a great Saviour. People come to me and ask me to pray with them about some failure, and then they begin to explain that they did not really mean to do it and that their purpose was all right. That is not facing things honestly with God. Some one tells of a woman who went to Charles Wesley and said, "I want you to pray for me. I am really a great sinner."

He stopped her and said, "Let us pray," and he began to pray, "O Lord, we pray for this poor sister. She is a great sinner."

She got so indignant and caught him by the arm and said, "Stop! who has been telling you about me?"

"I was just saying what you yourself told me."

People like to excuse themselves, but the great Saviour delights to reveal Himself to great sinners. "O Lord, pardon mine iniquity; for it is very great." Do not try to excuse it; do not try to minimize it. Let it appear at its worst, and He is there at once to deal with you in grace.

In verses 12 to 15 you get the soul's expression of trust and confidence, "What man is he that feareth the Lord [the one who stands in awe before God, who approaches Him reverently]? him shall He teach in the way that He shall choose. His soul shall dwell at ease; and his seed shall inherit the earth."

And now verse 14 contains a very wonderful truth, "The secret of the Lord is with them that fear Him; and He will shew them His covenant." The secret of the Lord is the covenant of grace, and He says that covenant of grace is with them that fear Him. He makes known His secret to those who stand in awe in His presence. "Mine eyes are ever toward the Lord; for He shall pluck my feet out of the net."

He closes the Psalm with another prayer, beginning with verse 16, "Turn Thee unto me, and have mercy upon me; for I am desolate and afflicted. The troubles of my heart are enlarged: O bring Thou me out of my distresses. Look upon mine affliction and my pain; and forgive all my sins." Just think of him fleeing from Absalom, all the pain and grief that is rending his heart, his own son having proven so unworthy. Is there anything that a father feels more than that? He pours out everything to God and does not attempt to justify himself and so pleads with God, "Forgive all my sins." And then he puts God between the enemy and himself, "Consider mine enemies; for they are many; and they hate me with cruel hatred. O keep my soul, and deliver me: let me not be ashamed; for I put my trust in Thee." It is the expression of absolute confidence in God. "Let integrity and uprightness preserve me; for I wait on Thee." I have no one else to whom I can turn, and so I wait on Thee.

"Redeem Israel, O God, out of all his troubles." You can see how beautifully these words will fit the lips of the remnant in the days of the great tribulation as they are waiting on God for deliverance from the power of the antichrist

The 26th Psalm continues the same subject but emphasizes separation to the Lord from the evil on every side, and so the soul calls upon God, "Judge me, O Lord; for I have walked in mine integrity: I have trusted also in the Lord; therefore I shall not slide." There is a sense of conscious uprightness. You cannot pray with assurance unless you have that. If you go to God about something and have not a good conscience you cannot pray. "If I regard iniquity in my heart, the Lord will not hear me" (Psa. 66:18). I have known what it was to go along, thinking everything was all right, and yet not have much realization of the presence of God, and suddenly I was called to a dear one in whom I was intensely interested, and who was suffering illness. The request had come, "Will you go and pray with this one?" And as I would kneel to pray the thought would come, I am not in a condition to pray. I have not been living close enough to the Lord. I have been too careless about things, letting things go instead of dealing with them before God, and so I could not pray. There would have to be a facing of failure before God, and only when I knew that things were dealt with could I pray with any sense of assurance. David is not boasting of any goodness but says to the One who knows all the secrets of the heart, "I have trusted also in the Lord; therefore I shall not slide," and then he cries, in case the Lord should see something he does not, "Examine me, O Lord, and prove me; try my reins and my heart." In other words, "I want Thee to search me through and through, and if there is anything hindering fellowship, anything keeping me from being on praying ground, make it manifest for I want to be right with Thee."

"For Thy lovingkindness is before mine eyes: and I have walked in Thy truth. I have not sat with vain persons." There has been conscious separation from the ungodly. "Neither will I go in with dissemblers. I have hated the congregation of evil doers; and will not sit with the wicked. I will wash mine hands in innocency: so will I compass Thine altar, O Lord." What offerings of praise and thanksgiving we would bring to God if every one of us, as we drew near His altar, could say, "Lord, I have washed mine hands in innocency—I have judged everything; I have been cleansed by the washing of water by the Word, so that I know of nothing in my heart or life that hinders communion with Thee." How we could pray and work and count on God to intervene! "So will I compass Thine altar, O Lord: That I may publish with the voice of thanksgiving, and tell of all Thy wondrous works."

And just as he has expressed his detestation of the evil doer he expresses his deep affection for the house of God, "Lord, I have loved the habitation of Thy house, and the place where Thine honour dwelleth. Gather not my soul with sinners, nor my life with bloody men." He cannot get near the house of God, and enemies are around him. "In whose hands is mischief, and their right hand is full of bribes. But as for me, I will walk in mine integrity: redeem me, and be merciful unto me. My foot standeth in an even place: in the congregations will I bless the Lord." And he looks on in faith believing that God is indeed going to give deliverance.

In Psalm 27 we have the saint's desire. What is it that the child of God desires above everything else? Is it not fellowship with the One who has redeemed him? And so here you have David exclaiming, "The Lord is my light and my salvation; whom shall I fear?" Let the enemy rage as he will; I will confide in God. "The Lord is the strength of my life; of whom shall I be afraid? When the wicked, even mine enemies and my foes, came upon me to eat up my flesh, they stumbled and fell. Though an host should encamp against me, my heart shall not fear: though war should rise against me, in this will I be confident." In what? That above everything else I have desired fellowship with Thee! "One thing have I desired of the Lord, that will I seek after." What is that one thing? Fellowship with God. "That I may dwell in the house of the Lord all the days of my life, to behold the beauty of the Lord, and to enquire in His temple." What does he mean by "the beauty of the Lord"? It is His moral beauty. We have never seen the face of the Lord. We have never looked upon His countenance, and yet we have seen His beauty because we have realized, as we have studied the Word, His moral and spiritual perfection.

Many years ago, on a car one day, a number of high school girls were laughing and chatting. A woman with a heavy veil over her face boarded the car, and as she got on the wind blew the veil aside and one could see that she had a terribly scarred face; it had evidently been badly burned. It looked horrible and one of these girls exclaimed, "Oh, look at that fright!" Another of the girls seeing who it was about whom they were speaking wheeled around and turned to the other in flaming anger and said, "How dare you speak of my beautiful mother in that way?"

"Oh, I am so sorry, I didn't think what I was saying. I did not mean to say anything unkind of your mother, I did not know it was your mother."

"Yes, it is," the other replied, "and her face is the most beautiful thing about her to me. Mother left me in my little crib when a small child and went to a store to get something. When she came back the house was on fire, and my mother fought her way through the fire and flames and wrapped me all up so that the flames could not reach me; but when she got outside again she fell down burned terribly, but I was safe. And whenever I look at her I think what a beautiful mother I have."

They say beauty is only skin deep. Moral beauty goes to the depths of the soul, and when David says that he wants to dwell in the house of the Lord to behold the beauty of the Lord, he means, I want to be taken up with the holiness and the love and the grace and the compassion of the Lord.

"In the time of trouble He shall hide me in His pavilion: in the secret of His tabernacle shall He hide me; He shall set me up upon a rock." Notice the different figures he uses. The foe all about but David is hidden in God's pavilion, in the innermost part of the tabernacle. The secret place would be the holiest of all. And then, "He shall set me up upon a rock"; and we know that the rock is Christ. "And now shall mine head be lifted up above mine enemies round about me: therefore will I offer in His tabernacle sacrifices of joy; I will sing, yea, I will sing praises unto the Lord. Hear, O Lord, when I cry with my voice: have mercy also upon me, and answer me." And now notice the heart's exercise, "When Thou saidst, Seek ye My face; my heart said unto Thee, Thy face, Lord, will I seek." What did you say when He said, "Seek ye My face"? Did you reply, "Some other time, Lord; I have too much to do now; I have my business, I have the housework to do and cannot bother with the Word now; some other time"? But David says, "When Thou saidst, Seek ye My face; my heart said unto Thee, Thy face, Lord, will I seek." As much as to say, Lord, I am so thankful that Thou desirest me to come into Thy presence. I am delighted to come; "Thy face, Lord, will I seek."

"Hide not Thy face far from me; put not Thy servant away in anger: Thou hast been my help; leave me not, neither forsake me, O God of my salvation. When my father and my mother forsake me, then the Lord will take me up." When the dearest ones on earth forsake me then the Lord will care for me. And so he continues to pray, "Teach me Thy way, O Lord, and lead me in a plain path, because of mine enemies. Deliver me not over unto the will of mine enemies: for false witnesses are risen up against me, and such as breathe out cruelty." Do you not see how this Psalm might be applied to the Lord Jesus Himself when He was here on earth? He could have taken these words on His lips, He could say to the Father, "When Thou saidst, Seek Ye My face; My heart said unto Thee, Thy face, Lord, will I seek." And when before Caiaphas, He could have said, "False witnesses are risen up against Me, and such as breathe out cruelty." And He left "us an example, that ye [we] should follow His steps."

The Psalm closes with these words, "I had fainted, unless I had believed to see the goodness of the Lord in the land of the living. Wait on the Lord: be of good courage, and He shall strengthen thine heart: wait, I say, on the Lord." God does not always do for us immediately what we ask. We are not only to wait on the Lord but also to wait for the Lord. Wait His own time. But now notice that thirteenth verse, "I had fainted, unless I had believed to see the goodness of the Lord in the land of the living." The words, "I had fainted" are in italics. There is nothing in the original to answer to them. But, you say, you would not have a complete sentence without them; you could not say, "Unless I had believed to see the goodness of the Lord in the land of the living." No, you could not have a declarative sentence, but you might have an exclamatory sentence like this, "Oh, if I had not believed to see the goodness of the Lord in the land of the living!" What a tragedy it would have been if I had not believed, what a terrible blunder I would have made if I had not believed in these difficult days! I have had numbers of Christian businessmen say to me, "Oh, my brother, if it had not been for my confidence in the Lord, when my business went to pieces and when the savings of the years were swept away, I would have been like those other people who went to one of these high buildings and jumped off." That is what David is saying, Oh, the tragedy if I had not known the Lord! But my soul was at peace and I could wait upon Him.

PRAYERS AND PRAISES
PSALMS 28 TO 31

IN THE 28TH Psalm WE HAVE GOD'S REMNANT PEOPLE celebrating known deliverance. They had been in difficulty, in trial, and God had intervened, and now they are praising Him for it and crying to Him that nothing might arise to hide His face, to make them insensible to His voice, that sin might not come in to mar their fellowship and communion with Him.

Notice the opening verse, "Unto thee will I cry, O Lord my rock; be not silent to me: lest, if Thou be silent to me, I become like them that go down into the pit." What does the Psalmist mean when he says, "Be not silent to me"? It is as though he said, "O God, do not let me be in a condition of soul where I cannot hear Thy voice." God is always speaking, but sometimes we become deaf to His voice, and so He seems to be silent to us. It is a solemn thing when a child of God can go on through this world day after day without ever hearing His voice. Have you heard it today? Has He spoken to you today?

We have a great movement sweeping parts of Great Britain, South America, India, Australia, New Zealand, and the United States and Canada, sometimes called the Oxford Group Movement. It is rather strange that it should be called by that name because it began in America. A certain pastor launched it some years ago on the eastern coast. This movement particularly emphasizes the importance of divine guidance. Unfortunately it lays no stress whatever on the importance of a second birth. Apparently it has nothing to say about redemption by the blood of the Lord Jesus Christ but a great deal about life changing and about confession and about listening to the voice of God. These terms sound very good, and they find answering assent in the hearts of many of God's beloved people. We are told that if we want to know whether there is a living God or not we should sit down quietly in the morning and try to let our mind become an absolute blank and then listen and let God speak. Whatever He tells you, as you hear the inward voice, do that thing.

It is a very unsafe thing for anybody to act on a principle like that. You say, well, what do you mean when you talk about hearing the voice of God? God speaks to us through His Word. If you want to hear the voice of God, sit down over your Bible and say, "Blessed Lord, as I read Thy Word let me hear Thee speaking to me." And if you know of anything in your life that is hindering fellowship with God, as the Spirit of God brings to your mind any unconfessed sin, any unjudged evil, you confess it, deal with that in the presence of God and remember, it is written, "If I regard iniquity in my heart, the Lord will not hear me" (Psa. 66:18). Now with everything put away as far as you know, turn to His Word and read it in dependence upon His Holy Spirit and if He does not speak, there is something wrong with you still.

David says, "Be not silent to me: lest, if Thou be silent to me, I become like them that go down into the pit." He would never go down into the pit, for he was saved from that; but he says as it were, The thing that I read is that if I am not in living touch with Thee, if I am not hearing Thy voice day by day, I know I will become just like the world around. A Christian out of fellowship with God does not cease to be a Christian, but he is not walking as a Christian should walk and so becomes "like them that go down into the pit."

"Hear the voice of my supplications, when I cry unto Thee, when I lift up my hands toward Thy holy oracle." And now we get a suggestion here of the difference between Old Testament worship and New Testament worship. The Old Testament saint knew nothing of what you and I through grace should know and understand. In all of the Old Testament dispensation God was hidden behind a heavy veil. He dwelt in the thick darkness and only the high priest could push that aside and enter once a year, bearing the blood of atonement. But now it is altogether different. The Old Testament saint said, "I lift up my hands toward Thy holy oracle." But what about the New Testament saint? Look at Hebrews 10:19–22 and see how different our position is, "Having therefore, brethren, boldness to enter into the holiest by the blood of Jesus, By a new and living way, which He hath consecrated for us, through the veil, that is to say, His flesh; And having an high priest over the house of God; Let us draw near with a true heart in full assurance of faith, having our hearts sprinkled from an evil conscience, and our bodies washed with pure water," or with "the water of purification," referring to the nineteenth chapter of the book of Numbers, undoubtedly. Look at the difference. The Old Testament saint was truly a child of God, truly forgiven, but he knew nothing of immediate access into the holiest because the veil was not yet rent. The precious blood of Christ had not yet been shed, and so these Psalms do not rise to the full height of New Testament worship. That is one reason why we need to be careful when we try to use them as vehicles of Christian praise, testimony, and adoration. The tone of worship never rises to New Testament heights until we enter into the holiest through the value of the precious blood of Jesus. The Old Testament saint says, "I lift up my hands toward Thy holy oracle." Suppose I were to try to sing that today. I will not do anything of the kind. The oracle was the holiest of all. I belong in the holiest of all. I enter, in all the infinite value of the precious atoning blood of Christ. On the other hand, a great many of the Psalms are beautiful expressions of praise and worship, but they all reach just a certain height. You get the full height of Christian worship in Revelation where we read, "Unto Him that loved us, and washed us from our sins in His own blood, And hath made us kings and priests unto God and His Father; to Him be glory and dominion for ever and ever" (Rev. 1:5, 6). I wish I could write music. I would like to write an anthem on those words, for that is what we are going to sing in Heaven.

The Psalmist recognizes that he is in the midst of enemies, and every believer must see that, and so David prays that he might not learn their ways—"Draw me not away with the wicked, and with the workers of iniquity, which speak peace to their neighbors, but mischief is in their hearts." You never saw anybody like that, did you? You never saw a person like that in your mirror, did you? We can be so soft and sweet and nice, and all the time mischief is in the heart David says, "I do not want to be like that." And then judgment is called down upon them. We would not call down judgment because we are living in the dispensation of grace; but this was in the dispensation of law.

In the latter part of the Psalm, David's heart goes out in thanksgiving and praise for deliverance. "Blessed be the Lord, because He hath heard the voice of my supplications. The Lord is my strength and my shield; my heart trusted in Him, and I am helped." Can you say that? "The Lord is my strength and my shield"? My strength to enable me to do the things that ordinarily I could not do; my shield to protect me from my foes. My conflict is not now with flesh and blood but with wicked spirits in heavenly places, and I need such a shield as this. "Therefore my heart greatly rejoiceth; and with my song will I praise Him. The Lord is their strength, and He is the saving strength of His anointed." That is, His Messiah. "Save Thy people, and bless Thine inheritance: feed them also, and lift them up for ever."

In the 29th Psalm we have the majesty of God celebrated. God is looked at here as the Sovereign Ruler of the universe. He has control not only of the hearts of men but also of nature. Everything is subject to Him. I do not know whether there is a finer poem in the Bible than this 29th Psalm. We do not always judge literature aright, but to me this Psalm is one of the loveliest poems that I have ever seen. I wonder whether you have ever noticed what it really is. It starts with an ascription of praise to God and then goes on to a description of a great storm moving in from the Mediterranean Sea and up toward the mountains of Lebanon. David, standing on the porch of his palace, looking out and watching that storm as it rages, realizes that "Jehovah standeth o'er the waterfloods." "Give unto the Lord, O ye mighty, give unto the Lord glory and strength. Give unto the Lord the glory due unto His name; worship the Lord in the beauty of holiness." Now you get something that New Testament saints may well enter into, for we cannot get beyond this, "Worship the Lord in the beauty of holiness."

As he is contemplating the glory of God, suddenly he hears the thunder roll and sees the lightning flash, and exclaims, "The voice of the Lord is upon the waters." He is looking out toward the Mediterranean. "The voice of the Lord is upon the waters: the God of glory thundereth." And now the rain begins to pour down. "The Lord is upon many waters." And still the thunder rages. "The voice of the Lord is powerful; the voice of the Lord is full of majesty." And now the storm moves on across the plain and up to the mountains of Lebanon, and the great trees crash as the lightning strikes them. "The Voice of the Lord breaketh the cedars; yea, the Lord breaketh the cedars of Lebanon. He maketh them also to skip like a calf; Lebanon and Sirion like a young unicorn"—really, a wild ox. As the wind seems to be tearing those great trees and they are swaying back and forth David sees them just like a lot of animals that are driven before the wind. And then as he notes the lightning flashing he cries, "The voice of the Lord divideth the flames of fire." Now the storm has moved on to the south and over to the wilderness of Judea, and still he is watching as he cries, "The voice of the Lord shaketh the wilderness; the Lord shaketh the wilderness of Kadesh. The voice of the Lord maketh the hinds to calve, and discovereth the forests: and in His temple doth every one speak of His glory." He thinks of the whole universe as a great temple of God. "And in His temple"—in His sanctuary—"doth every one speak of His glory." That might be rendered, "In His sanctuary everything expresses His glory." That was true of the tabernacle, and it was true of the temple, these lesser sanctuaries, for everything in them was divinely ordered and every board and every stone and every curtain and every bit of furniture spoke of His glory. As you study the tabernacle or the temple you find that it expresses Christ throughout, for God's glory is all summed up in Christ.

"The Lord sitteth upon the flood: yea, the Lord sitteth King for ever." Now the storm is dying away and all nature is quiet again, and David says, "The Lord will give strength unto His people; the Lord will bless His people with peace." What a contrast! The Psalm begins with the rolling thunder, the roaring winds, and the flash of lightning but now all is quiet. It is a wonderful picture of the soul that has gone through its exercises, its stress, its trouble but has learned that God is over all, that He is strong to save. And so the heart rests in Him and is at peace.

The next five Psalms of this special division, 30 to 34, are Psalms of salvation. They all set before us, in their different ways, experimental salvation, the personal knowledge that comes to those who trust the Lord for His delivering grace. In Psalm 30 David is praising God for this salvation. Notice it says at the top, "A Psalm and Song at the dedication of the house of David." This is suggestive, if it is correct, and it probably is, for those headings really belong in the Hebrew texts. It would indicate that when David built a house for himself to dwell in he had a dedication of the house, and on that occasion he wrote this Psalm, and it was sung. As he looked back over the years he remembered how wonderfully God had undertaken for him; he thought of what he once was, an unknown shepherd boy, and then of the great victories God had given him in the midst of persecution, the wonderful way the Lord had watched over him and preserved his life, and then had made him King in Israel and given him this restful home. In it all David sees evidence after evidence of God's wonderful grace and compassion, and so he lifts his voice in adoration.

"I will extol thee, O Lord; for Thou hast lifted me up, and hast made my foes to rejoice over me." We like to sing about that today—"He lifted me." David was once down in the miry clay, but God had raised him in grace. "O Lord my God, I cried unto Thee, and Thou hast healed me. O Lord, Thou hast brought up my soul from the grave: Thou hast kept me alive, that I should not go down to the pit." His heart is so full he calls upon his brethren to join with him in thanksgiving, "Sing unto the Lord, O ye saints of His, and give thanks at the remembrance of His holiness."

Then he thinks of those days when he was so troubled, when he was hunted like a partridge upon the mountain, when his enemies were seeking his life day and night, when he was driven out from the haunts of men and he had to live in dens and caves, when many a night he sobbed and wept as he thought of the enmity of King Saul and realized that those he loved had turned against him. Now it is all in the past, and God has done such wonderful things, and he says, "His anger endureth but a moment; in His favour is life: weeping may endure for a night, but joy cometh in the morning." Does it not remind you of that passage in the fourth chapter of the Second Epistle to the Corinthians where we read, "For all things are for your sakes, that the abundant grace might through the thanksgiving of many redound to the glory of God. For which cause we faint not; but though our outward man perish, yet the inward man is renewed day by day. For our light affliction, which is but for a moment, worketh for us a far more exceeding and eternal weight of glory" (verses 15–17). What did David say? "His anger endureth but a moment; in His favour is life: weeping may endure for a night, but joy cometh in the morning." I wonder whether you are saying, "It seems it has been a long moment for me. I have had suffering and sorrow and disappointment and distress, and I have prayed about it but do not seem to get any answer, and it has gone on and on and on. Talk about a moment, I have had a lifetime of it." Oh yes, but if you know the Lord Jesus Christ, when this life is over, then what? Then eternity with Him! It will seem like just a moment. My mother told me that when my dear father was dying he was suffering terribly and a friend of his leaned over him and said, "John, you are suffering terribly, aren't you?"

"Oh," he said, "I am suffering more than I thought it was possible for any one to and live, but one sight of His blessed face will make up for it all."

And so whatever we are called upon to endure here, whatever we are called upon to suffer here it is for only a moment, comparatively. "Weeping may endure for a night, but joy cometh in the morning." Because the morning will be when Jesus returns. He says, "I am the bright and morning star," and His coming heralds the morning and then no more suffering, no more pain, no more sorrow.

Turning back to our Psalm we find that David reminds his own soul of his confidence in early days. He says, "In my prosperity I said, I shall never be moved." Did you ever say that before the depression began? You were piling up a nice little sum; you had some stocks and bonds and a paying business, and you said, "My, I have things in good shape; no danger now of not being well provided for in old age." Then suddenly everything was swept away. But God was not swept away. God abides just the same, and Jesus Christ is "the same yesterday and today and for ever" (Heb. 13:8). David, like Job, had said in his prosperity, "I shall never be moved," and then trouble came unexpectedly and from the most amazing source. The very last person in the world that he ever expected trouble to come from was King Saul, and yet he turned to be his enemy, moved by that frightful passion, jealousy, one of the most detestable passions of human nature. But the Lord undertook, and David now can say, "Lord by Thy favour Thou hast made my mountain to stand strong: Thou didst hide Thy face, and I was troubled." There were times when he tried to pray but could not see and could not realize God's presence. You have felt that way, have you not? Sometimes God does withdraw His face temporarily. Rutherford says,

"But flowers need night's cool darkness,
The moonlight and the dew.
So Christ from one who loved Him,
His presence oft withdrew."

The Lord knows that sometimes it is good for us to have these times of darkness, these times of difficulty. When He seems to us to be afar off He wants to teach us to trust in the dark as well as in the light. "I cried unto thee, O Lord; and unto the Lord I made supplication."

Now you get his prayer, for he feels as though his enemy is going to destroy him. "What profit is there in my blood, when I go down to the pit? Shall the dust praise Thee? Shall it declare Thy truth?" That is, my dead body, "shall it declare Thy truth? Hear, O Lord, and have mercy upon me: Lord, be Thou my helper." This is the way he prayed, but now listen to the way he praises, "Thou has turned for me my mourning into dancing: Thou has put off my sackcloth, and girded me with gladness; to the end that my glory may sing praise to Thee, and not be silent. O Lord my God, I will give thanks unto Thee for ever." Do you notice what David calls his tongue? His "glory." Did you ever notice what James calls it? Look at James 3:8. There is a rather remarkable contrast here. "The tongue can no man tame; it is an unruly evil." Have you a tongue like that? That is the uncontrolled tongue, but when God Himself controls it, David can call it his "glory." "To the end that my glory may sing praise to Thee." As much as to say, I am so glad I have a tongue that I can use to glorify Thee. If we used the tongue for that purpose all the time how different it would be.

We shall look briefly at the thirty-first Psalm. There we have a picture that links with the experience of our Lord Jesus Christ as well as with the individual saint. It is a Psalm in which the believer is showing his trust and confidence in God, rejoicing in His mercy, praising Him for His goodness, yet looking back to days of darkness and thanking God for deliverance.

"In Thee, O Lord, do I put my trust; let me never be ashamed: deliver me in Thy righteousness." The word translated "deliver" is exactly the same as the word for "save" so that this verse may be translated, "Save me in Thy righteousness." That is the only way God will save anybody. I always call this Martin Luther's verse. When he was a monk in the Augustinian monastery he was in great distress about his soul, and he tried by all kinds of penances to make some sort of atonement for his own sins, but he became more and more miserable and distressed. Then one day he was reading the Latin psalter and came upon this verse, "In Thee, O Lord, do I put my trust; let me never be ashamed: save me in Thy righteousness," and Luther stopped and looked at it and said, "What a strange verse. I can understand how God can damn me in His righteousness; how He can banish me from His presence in His righteousness for my sin deserves that; but if He saves me, surely He must save me in His mercy, not in His righteousness." But there was the word, "Save me in Thy righteousness," and Luther began mulling it over in his mind. He was led to turn to the Epistle to the Romans and read, "I am not ashamed of the gospel of Christ: for it is the power of God unto salvation to every one that believeth; to the Jew first, and also to the Greek. For therein is the righteousness of God revealed from faith to faith: as it is written, The just shall live by faith" (Rom. 1:16, 17). Not the mercy of God, merely, not the grace of God, simply, but the *righteousness* of God. The gospel shows how God can be righteous and yet justify ungodly sinners; and here, David, hundreds of years before the Cross, looks on in faith to the coming of the Saviour and says, "In Thee, O Lord, do I put my trust; let me never be ashamed: save me in Thy righteousness. Bow down Thine ear to me; deliver me speedily: be Thou my strong rock, for an house of defence to save me." And then faith leads him to say, "Thou art my rock and my fortress; therefore for Thy name's sake lead me, and guide me," and he calls on God to pull him out of the net. In verse 5 we have the words used by the Lord Jesus Christ when He hung upon the Cross, "Into Thine hand I commit My spirit" The Lord used these very words, showing us that He applied at least a part of the Psalm to Himself, to His own experience as He hung there upon that Cross bearing judgment due to sin.

Then look at verse 11 and again we can hear the Saviour speaking, "I was a reproach among all Mine enemies, but especially among My neighbours, and a fear to Mine acquaintance: they that did see Me without fled from Me. I am forgotten as a dead man out of mind: I am like a broken vessel." That is what Jesus is to the world, just as a dead man out of mind. If He ever lived, well, He is dead, gone the way of all flesh. One day there came into my book room in

Oakland a gentleman whom I did not know at first. He asked for a Bible, and when he told me the particular type of Bible he wanted I rather suspected that he was what we call a Christian Scientist. They generally use the Bible without these turn-over edges. I said, "You want the binding that matches Mrs. Eddy's 'Science and Health,' I presume."

"Yes," he said; "I am the first reader of such and such a Christian Science Church in the city."

I said, "Do you love that Book?"

"Oh yes; we read this in all our services. I read a portion from this Book, and the other reader reads a portion from Mrs. Eddy's 'Science and Health.' The two agree very much."

I said, "What is the precious blood of Jesus to you?"

I never saw a man turn so angry over a simple question. He flared up; his face worked convulsively for a moment or two, and then his fist came down on my desk, and he said, "The blood of Jesus! It is nothing more to me than the blood of any other dead Jew."

That is just what the Word of God says, "Forgotten as a dead man out of mind." Oh, the blasphemy of it. I said, "Well, that is what you say about the blood. Do you know what God says of it? 'The *precious* blood of Christ.' "

What do you say? Is it precious to you, or is Christ to you "forgotten as a dead man out of mind"?

Notice one or two verses in the latter part of this Psalm. You have often used the words of verse 15, "My times are in Thy hand." Do you really mean that? Is it not precious to know that "my times are in Thy hand"?

> *"My times are in Thy hand;*
> *Father, I wish them there;*
> *A father's hand can never cause*
> *His child a needless tear."*

And so one can just trust everything to Him, knowing that He will bring out all to His glory.

Then verse 19, "Oh how great is Thy goodness, which Thou hast laid up for them that fear Thee; which Thou hast wrought for them that trust in Thee before the sons of men!" You may not see it now but it will all come out eventually. "Thou shalt hide them in the secret of Thy presence from the pride of man: Thou shalt keep them secretly in a pavilion from the strife of tongues."

THE BLESSED MAN
PSALM 32

IN THE FOURTH CHAPTER OF THE EPISTLE TO THE ROMANS when the Apostle Paul is establishing the great doctrine of justification by faith alone, he cites two Old Testament scriptures as proof that in all dispensations every one who was ever saved was saved by grace through faith, altogether apart from human merit. In the third chapter, verse 21, we read, "But now the righteousness of God without the law is manifested, being witnessed"—or borne testimony to—"by the law and the prophets." Those terms, "The law and the prophets," refer not to individuals so much, but to the two divisions of the Old Testament. The books of Moses were called by the Hebrews "the Law." All the rest of the books, beginning with Joshua and running right on to the end, they called "the Prophets." Sometimes they divided the second group into three and called them "the Former Prophets" (that is, the early historical books all written by prophets) and then "the Writings" (books like Job, Psalms, Song of Solomon, etc.), and "the Latter Prophets," from Isaiah to Malachi. What the Apostle Paul is telling us in the third chapter of Romans is that upon the proven unrighteousness of all men, God is making known His righteousness which He Himself has provided for guilty sinners, which is not based on obedience to the law of Moses, but yet is borne witness to by the Law, those first five books, and by the Prophets, all the remaining books of the Old Testament. In other words, the entire Old Testament bears witness to the fact that God was going to bring His righteousness near to men who had none of their own.

If we had an orthodox Jew here, one thoroughly familiar with his Bible and the history of his people, and we said to him, "Who is the most important person in all the books of the Law?" he would answer without a moment's hesitation, "Abraham, because Abraham was the father of the Hebrew people, and the one with whom God made the covenant of grace." Very well, the Apostle Paul says in the fourth of Romans, let us take the most important person out of the books of the Law and see how he is justified, and he cites Abraham and says that the Scripture declares that "Abraham believed God, and it was counted unto him for righteousness" (verse one). That was justification by faith; that was righteousness apart from works.

Then if we had this orthodox Jew here and were to say to him, "Who is the most important personage mentioned in all the other books of the Old Testament, the Prophets?" He would answer without a moment's hesitation, "Our great King David, because God confirmed His covenant with David saying, 'I will give you the sure mercies of David,' and Messiah is to come through David's line." Well, the apostle says in the fourth of Romans, let us call in the most important man in the books of the Prophets and see how he was justified, see what he has to say about the way a guilty sinner finds life and peace, and so he quotes from the thirty-second Psalm. "Even as David also describeth the blessedness of the man, unto whom God imputeth righteousness without works, saying, Blessed are they whose iniquities are forgiven, and whose sins are covered" (Rom. 4:6, 7). He refers us to the thirty-second Psalm as the outstanding scripture setting forth the way God justifies ungodly sinners. And so when we turn back to consider it we find that it fits in wonderfully with the New Testament opening up of the gospel of the grace of God.

When Augustine of Hippo was dying, he had somebody paint this Psalm in large letters on a big placard, and he kept it right at the foot of his bed. As he lay there he had those beautiful words before him and went out into eternity dwelling upon the message of this thirty-second Psalm. It was one of Luther's favorite Psalms, because it sets forth the gospel more clearly perhaps than any other Old Testament scripture except the fifty-third chapter of the book of the prophet Isaiah.

In the first two verses of the Psalm we have the consummation. That is a peculiar thing about the structure of many of these Psalms. Often you get the climax in the very beginning and then in the verses that follow, the Psalmist, guided by the Holy Spirit, shows how it was reached. So here in the first two verses you have the fourfold blessedness of the believer, and in the rest of the Psalm you learn how David was brought into the enjoyment of this blessedness. We know that it was David, because we have the inspired heading, "A Psalm of David," and after that you have an untranslated Hebrew word, "Maschil." This word literally means, "giving instruction." It links with the statement found in the twelfth chapter of Daniel, "They that be wise among the people shall instruct many." The expression "they that be wise" is really in Hebrew, *the Maskilim*, i.e., "the instructors"; and so this Psalm is a Maschil Psalm, a Psalm giving instruction. Whenever reading the book of Psalms you come across that word, you will be wise if you say to yourself, "I must read this portion with special care because God is calling my attention to it by putting that word at the top. There is some special instruction here that He does not want me to miss"; and as we go into it we can see what that instruction really is.

Notice first the fourfold blessedness. "Blessed is he whose transgression is forgiven." That is the first thing. "Whose sin is covered." That is the second. "Blessed is the man unto whom the Lord imputeth not iniquity." That is the third. "And in whose spirit there is no guile." That is the fourth. The Hebrews called this an "Asher Psalm." The name of one of the tribes of Israel was called Asher. It means "happy" or "blessed," and we have a number of Psalms beginning with this word in the Hebrew. The first Psalm begins with that word, "Blessed is the man that walketh not in the counsel of the ungodly." The blessing of the first Psalm is the blessing of the Man who never went astray. You and I cannot claim that blessing. The blessed Man of Psalm 1 is our Lord Jesus Christ, no one else. Now we see that Psalm 32 is another Asher Psalm, but here we get the blessing of the man who did go astray but has been brought back to God; and you and I may know the blessedness of that. "Blessed is he whose transgression is forgiven." Who is that man? He is the man who has come to God owning his guilt and putting his trust in the message that God has given. In Old Testament times that message was not as full, as complete as the message that He has given today. Today He gives us the full, clear gospel of His own blessed Son who died for our sins; and when we put our trust in Him we know that through what Jesus did on Calvary all our iniquities are forgiven. The Apostle Peter makes that very plain when he says, "To Him give all the prophets witness, that through His name whosoever believeth in Him shall receive remission of sins" (Acts 10:43). Remission, of course, is forgiveness, and so we receive forgiveness of sins through believing in the Lord Jesus Christ. Every poor sinner who believes what God has testified concerning His Son is forgiven.

But notice the second thing: "Blessed is he ... whose sin is covered." This word translated "covered" is just one form of the word that is used throughout the Old Testament for "atonement." What he is really saying here is this, "Blessed is he whose sin is atoned for." The real meaning of "atonement" is "covering." God found a covering for sin when He gave the Lord Jesus Christ to die in our room and stead, and so now He says, "Blessed is he whose sin is covered." The precious blood blots out all the record, and his sin is covered.

Then look at the third thing, "Blessed is the man unto whom the Lord imputeth not iniquity." What is it to impute iniquity? It is to mark iniquity down. If the Lord Jesus blotted out all my sins the night He saved me and immediately began putting down more against me, I would not be much better off in the future than in the past but the Psalmist says, "Blessed is the man unto whom the Lord imputeth not iniquity." God is not marking down sin against His people as something they must face in the day of judgment. The moment I trust in Jesus, the precious blood covers the whole record from the cradle to the grave. Does that mean that I can sin and it does not make any difference? No, the moment my responsibility as a sinner having to do with the God of judgment ended for eternity, my responsibility as a child having to do with my Father began. I will never have to do with the God of judgment again, but I do have to do with my Father, and as a child I am to be an obedient child. If a naughty child, my Father will have to whip me for it. "Whom the Lord loveth He chasteneth, and scourgeth every son whom He receiveth" (Heb. 12:6). But He never imputes iniquity to His people. Instead of imputing iniquity He imputes righteousness. Every believer is made the righteousness of God in Christ.

Then look at the fourth thing. "Blessed is the man ... in whose spirit there is no guile." A man in whose spirit there is no guile is not a sinless person. There are no sinless people on earth. There was one and that was our blessed Lord Jesus Christ, but since the fall of Adam there has never been another. "All have sinned, and come short of the glory of God" (Rom. 3:23). There is not a just man that doeth good and sinneth not. "In many things we offend all." This is true of believers as well as of unbelievers. Even believers offend in many things but the man in whose spirit there is no guile is the man who is not trying to cover up and hide. He has owned up that he is just what God says he is. As long as a man is covering his sin, there is guile there. When David kept on covering his sin there was guile but when David came out frankly and acknowledged it and said, "I have sinned against the Lord," there was no more guile.

Years ago in Great Britain there was a young man working in a counting house. He sat on one of those high old-fashioned stools and worked on his books. He was a very nervous young man. Every time the door would open he wanted to see who was coming in. When he got ready to go out at noon or at night he would go to the door and open it and look up and down the street, and if he saw a military man or a police officer he would dodge back until they passed. One day while at work another of the clerks stepped over to him and leaning across the desk said, "I say, Jock, I am not making enough to keep me going as I live; let me have a couple of shillings to tide me over the week."

"I cannot do it," said Jock, "my wages are so small."

"Well, let me tell you something," and he whispered in his ear.

Poor Jock turned pale, reached in his pocket and said, "For God's sake, don't tell anybody!"

The other fellow, walking away, said to himself, "Well, I guess I have struck a silver mine," and every week or so he would come back and say, "Let me have a half crown" or something like that, and poor Jock gave it to him, till he was almost destitute himself.

One day, sitting in a little restaurant where he went for a cup of tea, Jock happened to notice a newspaper in another man's hand and he saw the heading, "Free pardon offered to all deserters of Her Majesty's Forces." "Oh," he said, "I must get that paper!" It was Queen Victoria's Jubilee, and they had decreed that in order to celebrate that date a free pardon should be granted to all deserters, but it went on to tell the terms of the pardon. The deserter must write in to headquarters, must tell what ship or regiment he belonged to, tell why he had deserted and give his present address, and if satisfactory, he would get a pardon. This was Jock's secret. He went home and wrote a letter to headquarters telling them that he was so glad to see that Her Majesty was giving a pardon to deserters, that he had not meant to be a deserter but when ordered to Egypt he was anxious to see his mother, and when he got back the ship was gone, etc. He waited. Then one day a large envelope was handed to him with the letters, O. H. M. S. How eagerly he opened it. There was just a curt little note. "Mr. So and So, Dear Sir, Your letter is received. Evidently you did not read the proclamation carefully. The pardon is for deserters but according to your letter you never intended to desert. Respectfully, General W." "What a fool I have been," said Jock. "I missed the pardon by trying to make out too good a case for myself." So he went home and sat down and wrote another letter: "I was attached to such and such a regiment. I deserted, and I can be found at such and such a place. If there is a pardon for me I will appreciate getting it." A few days later along came another large envelope. He opened it and was just looking at the paper it contained when his tormentor slipped up and said, "I say, Jock, I haven't had anything from you for a week."

"You have had the last bit of silver you will get from me," said Jock.

"Oh, we are getting awfully highty-tighty all of a sudden. If it isn't worth your while to keep me quiet I can tell your secret."

"Go and tell everybody you like; shout it everywhere. Tell them I am a deserter. Tell them all about it."

"Are you going crazy?"

"No; I am not, but before you go and tell them, read this," and he held the letter up: it was a free pardon.

"Oh, I guess my silver mine is dried up," said the other.

Jock now was a man in whose spirit there was no guile. All through those weary months he had been hiding, covering up, covering up, covering up, but there was nothing now to hide. It is a good thing when everything is out between you and God. "Blessed is the man … in whose spirit there is no guile."

In the next three verses David tells how he got to know this. He first tells of the time he did not know it. "When I kept silence, my bones waxed old through my roaring all the day long." If there is anything on earth that will make you feel like an old man it is unconfessed sin, trying to be so nice outside while inside there is such a roaring going on. For day and night Thy hand was heavy upon me: my moisture is turned into the drought of summer." Just like the burning hills, so green and beautiful in winter, so dried up in summer. All his joy was gone; he was desolate, and he could not stand it any longer, and so he says, "I acknowledged my sin unto Thee, and mine iniquity have I not hid." He had been hiding it, but it brought him nothing but sorrow.

"I said, I will confess my transgressions unto the Lord." And the very next thing is a free pardon, "And Thou forgavest the iniquity of my sin." Have you been there? "If we confess our sins, He is faithful and just to forgive us our sins, and to cleanse us from all unrighteousness" (1 John 1:9). Now everything is different. Now he is on praying ground. A lot of people think it is necessary to pray in order to be saved. David says, I could not pray in those old days, but I can now. For this shall every one that is godly pray unto Thee in a time when Thou mayest be found: surely in the floods of great waters they shall not come nigh unto him." Because he knows what it is to be forgiven, because he knows what it is to be without guile, he can pray with glad, happy assurance and know that the Lord will protect him in every time of trial.

See how beautifully he expresses himself in verse 7, "Thou art my hiding place; Thou shalt preserve me from trouble; Thou shalt compass me about with songs of deliverance," In verses 3 and 4 David was hiding *from* God, but in verse 7 he is hiding *in* God. Which are you doing? It makes such a difference. Some of us remember when we were hiding from God and were so miserable and unhappy, and then instead of hiding from Him we turned roundabout face and went directly to Him to find our hiding place in Him.

"Rock of Ages, cleft for me,
Let me hide myself in Thee;
Let the water and the blood,
From Thy wounded side which flowed,
Be of sin the double cure,
Cleanse me from its guilt and pow'r."

In the next three verses you hear the Lord speaking to David. David has been speaking so far, but now God speaks, and first He promises guidance. He says, "I have forgiven you, now I will undertake for you and will guide you through this scene—'I will instruct thee and teach thee in the way which thou shalt go: I will guide thee with Mine eye.' " Or, "with Mine eye upon thee." In another place we read, "As the eyes of a maiden [look] unto the hand of her mistress; so our eyes wait upon the Lord, our God" (Psa. 123:2). In other words, if you live in such close fellowship with God that you can always see His face, He will show you just how to go, and you won't be left to blunder. The reason people have such difficulty getting the mind of the Lord is that they know so little of what it is to live in fellowship with Him. "If therefore thine eye be single, thy whole body shall be full of light" (Matt. 6:22).

"Be ye not as the horse, or as the mule, which have no understanding: whose mouth must be held in with bit and bridle, lest they come near unto thee." How do you guide a horse or a mule? With your eye? Oh, no; "Whose mouth must be held in with bit and bridle, or they will not come near thee" (R. V.). A lot of Christians have to have bit and bridle guidance, because they will not keep their eyes on Jesus. The difference between a horse and a mule is, the horse gets the bit in his teeth and says, "I will," and you have a hard job to hold him back. The mule plants his feet and says, "I won't." You will find these two kinds of folk in the Christian Church. Many of them are just like a horse, ready to run away any time with anything you trust them with. They do not want to be guided or directed but off they go when only half prepared. But there are others—and they are the hardest to handle—who get so well established that you cannot move them. It is not lawful to use a whip to them. God says, Do not be like that.

And then a little word of warning, "Many sorrows shall be to the wicked." If men will not come to God and judge their sins, if they will not come and confess their wrong, if they will not get right with God, then they have to face grief and pain. They are bringing it upon their own heads. "But he that trusteth in the Lord, mercy shall compass him about." "Mercy enwraps him on every side," it may be translated.

And so he concludes with a song of praise, "Be glad in the Lord, and rejoice, ye righteous: and shout for joy, all ye that are upright in heart."

A Call to Worship
Psalm 33

IN THE THIRTY-SECOND PSALM DAVID CELEBRATES THE blessedness of the man whose transgression is forgiven and whose sin is atoningly covered. We have now in the thirty-third Psalm that which should always follow the knowledge of redemption—the heart going out to God in worship and adoration. You remember what the Lord Jesus Christ said to the woman at the well, "God is a Spirit: and they that worship Him must worship Him in spirit and in truth." "For the Father seeketh such to worship Him" (John 4:24, 23). Have you ever thought much of that? The Father is seeking worshipers. We know whom the Son is seeking. We read, "The Son of man is come to seek and to save that which was lost" (Luke 19:10). The Lord Jesus is seeking lost sinners, seeking them in order that He might save them; but among those who are already saved the Father is seeking worshipers. It is amazing how few believers know very much about worship, how few of them take the time to worship. Many people have such confused ideas of what worship is. You go to prayer meeting, spend the time in prayer and testimony and go away and say, "We were worshiping God tonight." But prayer is not worship; testifying is not worship. You go to listen to the Word preached and expounded and go away and say, "I have been down to worship God." But exposition of the Scripture is not worship; listening to the preaching is not worship. It is perfectly true that all these exercises ought to produce worship, for when we pray and we have such a wonderful sense of the nearness of God, that should lead our hearts out in adoration. That is what worship is: it is the soul's adoration of God Himself. It is occupation not with His gifts, not coming to Him to receive something, but occupation with the Giver, the heart going out in gratitude not only for what He has done for us but also for what He is in Himself. I never like to start the day but that I take a little time to sit quietly over the Word of God, and I seek to lift my heart to God, not to ask Him for things, but to tell Him a little of how I appreciate His wonderful love and His grace, the goodness that He has lavished upon me as a sinner, and then to adore Him for what He is in Himself. I find that the day seems brighter for a little time spent like that.

In Psalm 32 we have man delivered from his sins. In Psalm 33 we have the heart going out to the Deliverer in worship. We know that David wrote Psalm 32. We do not know who wrote Psalm 33. The Jews called the psalms that do not have any names at the head of them, Orphan Psalms. You say, "But are they not all by David?" They are called the Psalms of David." They are the Psalms of David in the sense that David was undoubtedly the first to put the collection together, but he did not write all the Psalms. The Jews used this book of Psalms as the expression of their worship, praise, thanksgiving, and their prayers in the synagogues and in the temple, but David did not write all of them. He included a great many Psalms written by writers whose names are not given. It is very remarkable the way the Psalms are arranged. They are arranged in divine order. In many instances we find the last verses of the one introducing the theme of the next. This Psalm is a case like that. The closing verse of Psalm 32 is this, "Be glad in the Lord, and rejoice, ye righteous: and shout for joy, all ye that are upright in heart." Now notice how the thirty-third Psalm starts, "Rejoice in the Lord, O ye righteous: for praise is comely for the upright."

The first three verses of this thirty-third Psalm are occupied with a call to praise the Lord, to worship Him. "Praise the Lord with harp: sing unto Him with the psaltery and an instrument of ten strings. Sing unto Him a new song." That is the song of redemption. "Play skilfully with a loud noise." In the temple of old they depended a great deal upon musical instruments. We may use them in our services today, but the instrument that God values above every other is that which the eye does not see nor the ears hear. The apostle says, "Singing and making melody in your heart to the Lord" (Eph. 5:19). And when your heart is attuned to God, when from the heart you are worshiping and praising, that is the sweetest music that ever reaches the ear of God. Sometimes people can sing very beautifully, they have trained voices and they never make a mistake in a note; everything is accurate, and yet there is not a particle in it for God. It is so easy to use talent and ability like that simply to attract attention to ourselves, just as it is easy to preach to glorify one's self and not God; but where the preacher's ability or the singer's ability is consecrated to God it is precious to Him. But even in a case where one cannot sing or play upon an instrument, if the heart is in tune and going out to Him in worship how precious it is to Jesus. He loves to find the hearts of His people occupied with Himself.

Then in verses 4 to 9 the soul contemplates God's Word and God's work. These are two witnesses to God. Creation and the Bible are both from the same source. Some people talk about the disagreement between the Bible and science. There is no disagreement between the Bible and science, that is, real science. Science consists of an orderly arrangement of proven facts explaining the universe, but where you simply get a lot of hypotheses that have never been proven that is not real science. Some of these may often be in conflict with the Bible, but never true science; because true science is simply the explanation of the physical universe, and the God who inspired the Bible made the universe. In this section of the Psalm you find the work and the Word of God testifying to His perfection.

"For the word of the Lord is right; and all His works are done in truth. He loveth righteousness and judgment: the earth is full of the goodness of the Lord." You need open eyes to see that. If your eyes are not open to see the goodness of the Lord, you can see so much to fill you with sorrow. There are trials wherever we look; there is suffering; there is disaster, but when you can look back of them all and realize that there is a God of love behind this universe, how it changes everything. "By the word of the Lord were the heavens made." That means, of course, the sun, the moon, and the stars. "And all the host of them by the breath of His mouth. He gathereth the waters of the sea together as an heap: He layeth up the depth in storehouses. Let all the earth fear the Lord: let all the inhabitants of the world stand in awe of Him." "Stand in awe," that is, a call to reverence. I think if there is one sin more than another that the people of God are guilty of in this country it is the sin of irreverence. You do not find it so much in some other lands. Cross the sea and go to Great Britain for instance. When people come together for the services of the Lord you do not find them rushing into churches and spending a lot of time in the foyer chatting and laughing, but they find their way quietly to their seats and bow in prayer as they wait for the service to begin. To me the shocking irreverence of American audiences is one of the hardest things to overcome. Sometimes it takes a half hour or so before one's spirit can get in tune for the meeting because of the noise and laughter and greeting one another that go on before the service. "Stand in awe, and sin not" (Psa. 4:4). "Let all the inhabitants of the world stand in awe of Him."

In verses 10 to 12 He is celebrated as the one true and living God in contrast to the idols of the heathen. "The Lord bringeth the counsel of the heathen to nought: He maketh the devices of the people of none effect. The counsel of the Lord standeth for ever, the thoughts of His heart to all generations." And now the writer of this Psalm speaks as a godly Israelite, grateful for the fact that God has revealed Himself to his people. "Blessed is the nation whose God is the Lord; and the people whom He hath chosen for His own inheritance." It is this holy nation of which the Apostle Peter speaks, that is made up of born again men and women everywhere all over the world. They constitute a nation of people that the Lord has set apart for Himself.

In verses 13 to 17 you have God weighing the hearts of men, looking down upon mankind and testing their thoughts. "The Lord looketh from heaven; He beholdeth all the sons of men. From the place of His habitation He looketh upon all the inhabitants of the earth. He fashioneth their hearts alike; He considereth all their works. There is no king saved by the multitude of an host: a mighty man is not delivered by much strength. An horse is a vain thing for safety: neither shall he deliver any by his great strength." God looks down upon mankind and what does He see? Just a world of weaklings, just poor, weak, sinful men unable to deliver themselves. But thank God He has a deliverance for them! And so in the last part of the Psalm, verses 18 to 22, you get God's care for His own. Out of this world He has chosen those who put their trust in Him, and He undertakes for them. "Behold, the eye of the Lord is upon them that fear Him, upon them that hope in His mercy, To deliver their soul from death, and to keep them alive in famine. Our soul waiteth for the Lord: He is our help and our shield. For our heart shall rejoice in Him, because we have trusted in His holy name. Let Thy mercy, O Lord, be upon us, according as we hope in Thee." It is a great thing for the soul to learn the meaning of that 20th verse, "Our soul waiteth for the Lord." It is one thing to wait *on* the Lord; it is another thing to wait *for* Him. David says, "My soul, wait thou only upon God; for my expectation is from Him" (Psa. 62:5). But here he says, "Our soul waiteth *for* the Lord." To wait on God means to come into His presence to worship Him, to adore Him, and to tell out your needs to Him, to bring your trials, difficulties, perplexities, tell them all to Him, wait on Him. But He does not always answer immediately. He does not always give instant deliverance. Perhaps you come to Him in sickness, and He does not always grant immediate healing. You come to Him in financial trouble, and He does not always give the means that you need to meet your responsibilities. You come to Him concerned about your family, maybe an unsaved one, a son, or daughter, wife, or husband, and you bring that one to God and talk to Him about him—you wait on the Lord. That is the right thing to do, but He may not always act immediately, and therefore we need to wait *for* Him as well as to wait *on* Him. Remember, if He does not answer immediately it does not mean that He is indifferent. God's delays are not denials. We need to learn that and to wait for the Lord, for in His own time and in His own way He undertakes and answers prayer. We cannot dictate to Him how or when He is to act.

THE RADIANT LIFE
PSALM 34

THE LAST PSALM OF THIS SECOND SERIES OF FIVE IS THE 34th, and again we find that it links with the one that went before. This previous Psalm has been calling people to worship, to praise Him, and the last two verses say, "For our heart shall rejoice in Him, because we have trusted in His holy name. Let Thy mercy, O Lord, be upon us, according as we hope in Thee." And immediately the soul speaks in the next Psalm, "I will bless the Lord at all times: His praise shall continually be in my mouth." Notice, this 34th Psalm, which presents Jehovah as the Deliverer, was written by David. We do not know who wrote Psalm 33, but are told distinctly who wrote Psalm 34, "A Psalm of David, when he changed his behaviour before Abimelech; who drove him away, and he departed." Do you remember that incident in David's life? He was afraid he was going to be slain by King Saul, and fled to the court of the Philistines and waited on the king of the Philistines. Just think, David who had overcome Goliath, the Philistine giant, became so discouraged that he lost his confidence, and instead of trusting God he fled to the enemies of his people and wanted to go with the Philistine king to battle, and would have gone out with them against his own people. How terribly David had fallen! There is no telling how far a saint of God will fall if he gets his eyes off the Lord, if unbelief triumphs instead of faith. Of course it will be only a temporary thing. The Philistines themselves said to Achish, King of Gath, "What are you doing with this fellow? This is the man who slew Goliath." But Achish said, "Oh, Saul has turned against him, and he is going to be my keeper now; he is going to fight for us." But they said, "We do not want this fellow around. If we go to battle he will turn against us." They knew that his heart was really with his own people, and they said, no, he cannot go. David was afraid, and we read, He "feigned himself mad in their hands, and scrabbled on the doors of the gate" (1 Sam. 21:13). What a picture! David, the man after God's own heart, God's anointed, feigning himself to be crazy because he was now afraid of the Philistines. Those orientals would never touch a lunatic, and so he pretended to be insane. What a disgusting picture! But no more disgusting than for you or me to go off with the world and act like the world—we who have been called out from it to glorify the Lord Jesus. God came in grace and delivered David from all that, and when he got back among his own people again he wrote this Psalm. David was delivered because Achish would not have him. He was feeling better now; he was back in the right place; he was delivered from the association of the Philistines.

Verses 1 to 4 are an ascription of praise. "I will bless the Lord at all times: His praise shall continually be in my mouth. My soul shall make her boast in the Lord: the humble shall hear thereof, and be glad. O magnify the Lord with me, and let us exalt His name together. I sought the Lord, and He heard me, and delivered me from all my fears." If only he had done that in the beginning he would not have failed so dreadfully in the palace of the king of the Philistines; but he had to have that bitter experience to bring him to an end of himself and to thrust him upon God. How often that happens to children of God.

In verses 5 to 10 you have a wonderful story of his own personal experience of the delivering power of God. That fifth verse has a marvelous lesson, "They looked unto Him, and were lightened: and their faces were not ashamed." "They looked unto Him." Unto whom? Unto the Lord. And what happened? "They were lightened: and their faces were not ashamed." Literally it means, "they became radiant." They looked unto Him, and became radiant: and their faces were not ashamed." Remember what the apostle tells us in the last verse of the third chapter of 2 Corinthians, "But we all, with open face beholding as in a glass the glory of the Lord, are changed into the same image from glory to glory, even as by the Spirit of the Lord." Do you want to become a radiant Christian? Do you want to be a Christlike believer? Then do not be self-occupied; do not be looking in all the time trying to see how you are getting along. If you are occupied with your bad self only, you will get discouraged; if occupied with your fancied goodness, you will get puffed up, but if you look away to Him, "Looking unto Jesus the author and finisher of our faith" (Heb. 12:2), what happens? "They looked unto Him, and became radiant." They not only received light themselves, but also they gave out light. Moses went into the presence of God, and when He came from the mount he was radiant; the people could not stand it. What made him radiant? He had been gazing on the face of God. If you want to be a radiant believer, fix your eyes upon Christ. "We all, [reflecting as in a mirror] the glory of the Lord, are changed into the same image from glory to glory" (2 Cor. 3:18). There is not a great deal of radiancy about some of us. We are so grumpy; we are so dull. The Scots have a good word for that; it is "dour," just glum, and it only tells the story that we are not looking unto Jesus. As we gaze upon His face we become like Him, and the loveliness of Christ shines out in our lives. "They looked unto Him, and became radiant: and their faces were not ashamed." David says, "I know, for I remember when I was not radiant but—this poor man cried, and the Lord heard him, and saved him out of all his troubles!" Can you say that?

And now David learned that he did not need to go to the Philistines for protection. God had a protector for him. "The angel of the Lord encampeth round about them that fear Him, and delivereth them." And he is so delighted at what he has found that he wants everybody else to share it with him and exclaims, "O taste and see that the Lord is good: blessed is the man that trusteth in Him. O fear the Lord, ye His saints." When he speaks of fearing the Lord he does not mean to be afraid of Him, but he means that reverent godly fear that should characterize us. "For there is no want to them that fear Him." If you are going about with head drooping all the time it tells the story that you are not living in His presence, for "There is no want to them that fear Him. The young lions do lack, and suffer hunger: but they that seek the Lord shall not want any good thing." There are many things that you and I think we want that are not good for us, but if we seek Him, if the Lord withholds something that we wanted very much, we can be sure it would not be a good thing for us.

It is a great thing to learn to depend on Him. That verse we quote so often does not promise that He will do every thing we ask, "Be careful for nothing; but in every thing by prayer and supplication with thanksgiving let your requests be made known unto God" (Phil. 4:6). And then what? And you will get everything for which you ask? No, "And the peace of God, which passeth all understanding, shall keep your hearts and minds through Christ Jesus" (Phil. 4:7). If you have told Him about it you can leave it with Him and be at perfect peace, and say, "I know that He will do the right thing." "They that seek the Lord shall not want any good thing." If He withholds that for which you are asking it is because He knows that it would not be for your good, and so He does not give it to you.

The last group of verses, from 11 to 16, give us the path of life for the believer. These words are quoted in the New Testament in 1 Peter 3:10 and on, "Come, ye children, hearken unto Me: I will teach you the fear of the Lord. What man is he that desireth life, and loveth many days, that he may see good? Keep thy tongue from evil, and thy lips from speaking guile." What had David been doing in the court of Achish? He had been speaking guile, and he got nothing but misery out of it. Now he is saying, if you want happiness and peace, "Keep thy tongue from evil, and thy lips from speaking guile. Depart from evil, and do good; seek peace, and pursue it. The eyes of the Lord are upon the righteous, and His ears are open unto their cry. The face of the Lord is against them that do evil." When Peter quotes this passage he stops right there but the Psalm continues, "The face of the Lord is against them that do evil, to cut off the remembrance of them from the earth." Why does Peter not quote that? Because this is not the day when God is cutting off the wicked; this is the day of grace. While the face of the Lord is against them that do evil He is still dealing with them in mercy, giving them a chance to be saved. The day of judgment has not yet come.

Verses 17 and 18 give us the experience of the trusting soul, The righteous cry, and the Lord heareth, and delivereth them out of all their troubles. The Lord is nigh unto them that are of a broken heart; and saveth such as be of a contrite spirit" What a lot of sad hearts there are in the world, and how the Lord loves to heal those hearts! "He healeth the broken hearted." Dr. Joseph Parker, one-time pastor in London, addressing a group of young theological students on preaching said, "Young gentlemen, always preach to broken hearts and you will never lack an audience." There are so many of them. The world is full of people with broken hearts and shattered hopes, but what a wonderful thing that "the Lord is nigh unto them that are of a broken heart"

The last few verses, 19 to 21, show the believer under the divine government, and the wonderful thing is that the Lord Jesus enters into this Himself. He was the broken hearted One when He was on the Cross. In the Old Testament we read, "In all their affliction He was afflicted, and the angel of His presence saved them" (Isa. 63:9). "Many are the afflictions of the righteous: but the Lord delivereth him out of them all. He keepeth all his bones: not one of them is broken." Do you remember when they came to break the legs of those men upon the crosses, they broke the legs of the one thief and then the other to hasten their death, but when they came to Jesus they saw He was dead already, so "they brake not His legs … that the scripture should be fulfilled" (John 19:33, 36). They did not know anything about the scripture, but it was there in the Word, "He keepeth all His bones: not one of them is broken. Evil shall slay the wicked: and they that hate the righteous shall be desolate. The Lord redeemeth the soul of His servants: and none of them that trust in Him shall be desolate."

Oh, that these Old Testament experiences might stir our hearts to lead us to get closer to our blessed Lord and thus farther away from the evil world that we too might become radiant as we are occupied with Him.

FELLOWSHIP WITH THE HOLY ONE
PSALMS 35, 36, AND 37

IN THIS SERIES OP PSALMS THE HOLINESS OF GOD IN GRACE and in judgment is specially emphasized. That is something I think we should all understand clearly. Everything that God does or everything that He permits is in accordance with His own holy nature. God will not allow anything either in the way of grace to sinners or in the way of trial to His people, or in the way of judgment falling upon the ungodly, that is contrary to the holiness of His nature. Only today somebody said to me, "I do not believe in the God of the Old Testament. I love the God and Father of our Lord Jesus Christ, but the God of the Old Testament is a God of judgment and vengeance and hatred, and I cannot believe in that God."

Our Lord Jesus Christ is the image of the invisible God. He is the exact expression of His character, and I do not see how any thoughtful person can fail to observe in reading the four accounts of the life of the Lord Jesus that the same things that are predicated of Jehovah in the Old Testament are seen in the Jesus of the New Testament. The Lord Jesus pronounces stern words of judgment. It is He who says, "Woe unto you, scribes and Pharisees, hypocrites." It is He who says of the cities in which the greatest of His mighty works had been done, "Woe unto thee, Chorazin! woe unto thee, Bethsaida! for if the mighty works, which were done in you, had been done in Tyre and Sidon, they would have repented long ago in sackcloth and ashes" (Matt. 11:21). He invokes judgment upon those cities because they rejected the light. And then it is He who speaks of the "worm [that] dieth not," "the fire [that] is not quenched," the wicked going "into everlasting fire, prepared for the devil and his angels." These expressions used by our Lord Jesus Christ are stronger than the ordinary expressions used of the judgment by the God of the Old Testament. And then again as far as vengeance is concerned we must remember when we think of God as a God of vengeance that we do not mean a revengeful God, but we mean that "Whatsoever a man soweth, that shall he also reap" (Gal. 6:7), and our Lord Jesus Christ insists upon the same thing. If men live in sin and wickedness and corruption, they are going to reap the results. God is going to take vengeance upon the wicked for their ungodly deeds. And if you say the God of the Old Testament is a God of hatred, so our Lord Jesus Christ has His hatreds too. The God of the Old Testament hated sin; He hated everything that was unholy, and our Lord Jesus Christ hates sin with a perfect hatred, and He loves holiness and loves purity. So it is all nonsense to try to differentiate between a God of the Old Testament and of the New. The God of the Old Testament said, "I have loved thee with an everlasting love" (Jer. 31:3), and the God of the New Testament said, "But God commendeth His love toward us, in that, while we were yet sinners, Christ died for us" (Rom. 5:8). So as we turn to these three Psalms we see God's way of grace and judgment shown to be in perfect accord with His infinite holiness.

In the thirty-fifth Psalm we have the soul in distress appealing to divine power for help, God recognized as the source of all blessing. Somebody has said, and I think rightly, that we may read this Psalm as the musings of the heart of Jesus as He stood before Pilate's judgment seat. Read it at your leisure with that thought in mind. Say to yourself, "I am going to think of this as though these words were uttered by the Lord Jesus as He stood before Pilate." And I think you will see how aptly they would fit just such a case. Of course there are certain expressions in it that our Lord Jesus Himself could not use, but the Psalm as a whole might well be a vehicle for expressing the thoughts of His heart. And we may think of it as a prayer which any tried saint, persecuted and misunderstood, might offer to God.

In the first six verses you have the soul's plea, "Plead my cause, O Lord, with them that strive with me: fight against them that fight against me. Take hold of shield and buckler, and stand up for mine help. Draw out also the spear, and stop the way against them that persecute me: say unto my soul, I am thy salvation." Can you not see how aptly the Lord Jesus could speak like this to the Father in that hour of trial? Can you not see how it would suit the lips of any troubled saint, persecuted and distressed, or how it fitted the lips of David when he was being hunted like a partridge on the mountain with Saul seeking his life? There is not necessarily any evil feeling in the heart, no unkind feeling when one in such a case calls upon God to confound his enemies. Would you not say the same today if in the circumstances of some of God's suffering people in China, if you had to flee from your home and had a wife and children with you and the enemy coming upon you? Do you not see how without any thought of hatred toward the people as such, but for the sake of those you love, you could pray, "Let them be confounded and put to shame that seek after my soul: let them be turned back and brought to confusion that devise my hurt. Let them be as chaff before the wind: and let the angel of the Lord chase them." Is that not beautiful? "Let the angel of the Lord chase them." I am not going to take vengeance into my own hands, but by Thy angels, O God, come between me and my foes and undertake for me!

Beginning with verse 7 and going on to verse 10 you have the troubled one pleading for help on the ground of conscious rectitude. When you have a good conscience toward God, when it is not accusing you, when you do not feel that the suffering you are going through is chastisement because of your own wrong doing, when you are clear in your own mind that you have been seeking to do the will of God, it gives you perfect confidence when you pray. And so the soul pleads like this, "For without cause have they hid for me their net in a pit, which without cause they have digged for my soul." Remember how the Lord quoted similar words from another Psalm, "They hated me without a cause." There He was, the holy One who had come with heart and hands full of blessing, and yet men turned upon Him with all their hatred and bitterness; but He could look up into the face of the Father and say, "O My Father, they hated Me without a cause," and so He pleads for judgment, "Let destruction come upon him at unawares; and let his net that he hath hid catch himself: into that very destruction let him fall. And My soul shall be joyful in the Lord: it shall rejoice in His salvation." Somebody may say, "Is that the New Testament spirit, to rejoice in the destruction of the enemy?" It is not that He is rejoicing in the destruction of the enemy but it is that He rejoices in the deliverance from the enemy. Take for instance that book, "A Thousand Miles of Miracles in China." When that dear missionary and his wife were fleeing from bandits, could they not pray like this, and if at last word came that the enemy had been destroyed would they not cry out with gladness, "My soul shall be joyful in the Lord: it shall rejoice in His salvation?" One is grateful for the deliverance, and of course in certain circumstances that deliverance necessarily means the destruction of the enemy. "All my bones shall say, Lord, who is like unto Thee, which deliverest the poor from him that is too strong for him, yea, the poor and the needy from him that spoileth him?"

And then in the next section, verses 11 to 18, we have the expression of the soul's absolute confidence in God. Perhaps there is no other part of the Psalm that could more fully express the heart of the Lord Jesus as He stood before Pilate than these words, "False witnesses did rise up; they laid to my charge things that I knew not. They rewarded me evil for good to the spoiling of my soul. But as for me, when they were sick, my clothing was sackcloth: I humbled my soul with fasting; and my prayer returned into mine own bosom. I behaved myself as though he had been my friend or brother: I bowed down heavily, as one that mourneth for his mother. But in mine adversity they rejoiced, and gathered themselves together: yea, the abjects gathered themselves together against me, and I knew it not; they did tear me, and ceased not." Think of the Lord Jesus when they took up stones to stone Him and He said, 'For which of those [good] works do ye stone Me?" In other words, "I have been among you doing nothing but good; I have sought only your blessing; why are you stoning Me?" And when they came to arrest Him in the garden He said, "When I was daily with you in the temple, ye stretched forth no hands against Me: but this is your hour, and the power of darkness" (Luke 22:53). And yet He had gone about doing good and healing all that were oppressed by the devil. There was no reason, from the human standpoint, why men should turn against Him; yet they hated Him because His holiness caused their sinfulness and wickedness to stand out in such a glaring light.

Again you hear him speak, "With hypocritical mockers in feasts, they gnashed upon me with their teeth." The gnashing of teeth expresses hatred. "Lord, how long wilt Thou look on? rescue my soul from their destructions, my darling from the lions. I will give Thee thanks in the great congregation: I will praise Thee among much people."

In the next group of verses, from 19 to 23, the soul now speaks to God of the sin, the wickedness of the adversary which in the very nature of things calls for judgment. We are so sentimental sometimes we forget that sin is the most hateful thing in all God's universe, and if sinners will not be separated from their sin they must be judged in and with their sin. And so we find here the Spirit of God speaking through that tried saint calling down judgment on the wicked. "Let not them that are mine enemies wrongfully rejoice over me: neither let them wink with the eye that hate me without a cause." These words definitely refer to the Lord Jesus.

"For they speak not peace: but they devise deceitful matters against them that are quiet in the land"—against them who are doing nothing to deserve such treatment. "Yea, they opened their mouth wide against me, and said, Aha, aha, our eye hath seen it. This Thou hast seen, O Lord: keep not silence: O Lord, be not far from me. Stir up Thyself, and awake to my judgment, even unto my cause, my God and my Lord."

And then in verses 24 to 28 the soul is at perfect peace as he leaves everything with God. Whatever comes, Lord, I turn it all over to Thee. It is a great thing to come to that place where you can truly trust and say, "I will trust, and not be afraid." "Judge me, O Lord my God, according to Thy righteousness; and let them not rejoice over me. Let them not say in their hearts, Ah, so would we have it: let them not say, We have swallowed him up. Let them be ashamed and brought to confusion together that rejoice at mine hurt: let them be clothed with shame and dishonour that magnify themselves against me. Let them shout for joy, and be glad, that favour my righteous cause: yea, let them say continually, Let the Lord be magnified, which hath pleasure in the prosperity of His servant. And my tongue shall speak of Thy righteousness and of Thy praise all the day long."

The next Psalm seems to fit in so aptly immediately following the 35th. It is also a Psalm of David. I do not know when he wrote it or under what circumstances, but he evidently had been musing on the different conditions of the wicked and the righteous; and so he undertakes in this Psalm to depict the sad state of the one and the joyous condition of the other. It seems to divide into just three parts. From verse 1 to 4 we have the estate of the wicked: "The transgression of the wicked saith within my heart, that there is no fear of God before his eyes." That is the thing that makes for wickedness, when men have absolutely cast off the fear of God. "For he flattereth himself in his own eyes, until his iniquity be found to be hateful. The words of his mouth are iniquity and deceit: he hath left off to be wise, and to do good. He deviseth mischief upon his bed; he setteth himself in a way that is not good; he abhorreth not evil." It is a very graphic description of the ungodly. Then in contrast to this we have the goodness of God toward the righteous. "Thy mercy, O Lord, is in the heavens; and Thy faithfulness reacheth unto the clouds. Thy righteousness is like the great mountains; Thy judgments are a great deep: O Lord, Thou preservest man and beast. How excellent is Thy lovingkindness, O God! therefore the children of men put their trust under the shadow of Thy wings."

While the wicked never find that for which they are seeking, never find peace, never find satisfaction, how different is the state of the righteous! "They shall be abundantly satisfied with the fatness of Thy house; and Thou shalt make them drink of the river of Thy pleasures." What is the river of God's pleasures? I think it is really the Holy Spirit's testimony to the preciousness of Christ. Did you ever drink of that river? Did you not get a wonderful draught?

Let us trace that river a bit through the Psalms. Look at Psalm 46:4, "There is a river, the streams whereof shall make glad the city of God, the holy place of the tabernacles of the most High." It is that refreshing stream that comes down from heaven to cheer and gladden the souls of those who drink. Then turn to Psalm 65:9, "Thou visitest the earth, and waterest it: thou greatly enrichest it with the river of God, which is full of water: Thou preparest them corn, when Thou hast so provided for it." And then you pass from the Psalms and get over to the book of Ezekiel and see that river flowing forth beneath the throne and the altar, the river of blessing to the whole world in millennial days. Then go to the book of Revelation and read, "And he shewed me a pure river of water of life, clear as crystal, proceeding out of the throne of God and of the Lamb" (Rev. 22:1), that wonderful river of which "if a man drinks he lives for ever." "Whosoever will, let him take the water of life freely" (Rev. 22:17). And the fountain of life is the Word of God made good to the soul by the Holy Spirit. As Jesus said to that woman at the well, "Whosoever drinketh of this water shall thirst again: But whosoever drinketh of the water that I shall give him shall never thirst; but the water that I shall give him shall be in him"—a fountain—not merely a well as we have it in our version—"of water springing up into everlasting life" (John 4:13, 14). David drank of this fountain, and we today who are saved enjoy the same blessing.

In the closing verses we see faith calling on God for complete deliverance, "O continue Thy lovingkindness unto them that know Thee; and Thy righteousness to the upright in heart. Let not the foot of pride come against me, and let not the hand of the wicked remove me. There are the workers of iniquity fallen: they are cast down, and shall not be able to rise." And yet perhaps as he wrote that he was still surrounded by his foes, but faith speaks of the things which are not as though they are. I can trust God, and the enemy will have no power against me.

We have seen many times how one Psalm links with another. Look at the 12th verse of the thirty-sixth Psalm and then look at the first verse of Psalm 37. Psalm 37 is God's answer to His people's cry. In these two Psalms we have had His people crying out to Him, and in the last verse of Psalm 36 we read, "There are the workers of iniquity fallen: they are cast down, and shall not be able to rise." Now look at the first verse of Psalm 37, "Fret not thyself because of evildoers, neither be thou envious against the workers of iniquity." The very same term that is used in the last verse of the previous Psalm is used in the first verse of the next Psalm. The troubled saint says, "Lord, I believe You are going to handle these workers of iniquity"; and then the Lord answers, "Don't you fret; you have turned it over to Me; I will take charge of you and will deal with them."

I wish we could depict this thirty-seventh Psalm as it is in the Hebrew. It is an alphabetical Psalm. Many people know that we have one marvelous alphabetical Psalm, the 119th. There are twenty-two sections, and every verse in each section begins with the same letter. In the twenty-two sections you have all the letters of the Hebrew alphabet; every verse, for instance, of the first section begins with Aleph which answers to our "A." We can easily see that because we get the names of the letters in the headings. The thirty-seventh Psalm is also an alphabetical Psalm, but here it is about every fourth line that begins with a different letter, and this runs through the twenty-two letters of the Hebrew alphabet. We will just take some of the outstanding features.

We have the Spirit's answer to the troubled soul, and so first in verses 1 to 11 we have blessing promised to the righteous. They are not to fret. God will deal with them. Verse 3 says, "Trust in the Lord, and do good"—that is your part. "So shalt thou dwell in the land, and verily thou shalt be fed. Delight thyself also in the Lord; and He shall give thee the desires of thine heart. Commit thy way unto the Lord; trust also in Him; and He shall bring it to pass. And He shall bring forth thy righteousness as the light, and thy judgment as the noonday. Rest in the Lord, and wait patiently for Him: fret not thyself because of him who prospereth in his way, because of the man who bringeth wicked devices to pass." Notice the definite command, "Trust in the Lord … delight thyself in the Lord … Commit thy way unto the Lord … Rest in the Lord … fret not thyself." You have often seen the little motto, "If you worry you do not trust; if you trust you do not worry." Somebody has written a beautiful little monograph entitled, "Why Worry When You Can Pray?"

The average person would rather worry than pray. It is our own fault that we worry so much, for it is because we do not pray more. If we would hand it over to Him, commit our way unto the Lord, it would be so different. But now again, "Trust in the Lord." My attitude of heart must be right. "Cease from anger, and forsake wrath: fret not thyself in any wise to do evil," and it will not be long before the wicked will disappear: God will deal with them. All the heaven they are ever going to know they get in this world, and all the trouble God's saints will know they are getting here. When you leave this scene the trouble will be left behind. Why not just thank Him and praise Him for all His delivering grace?

"But the meek shall inherit the earth; and shall delight themselves in the abundance of peace." When the day comes that God shall manifest His loving favor to the righteous and they have entered at last into their reward, what about the wicked? Look at verses 12 to 15, "The wicked plotteth against the just, and gnasheth upon him with his teeth. The Lord shall laugh at him: for He seeth that his day is coming. The wicked have drawn out the sword, and have bent their bow, to cast down the poor and needy, and to slay such as be of upright conversation. Their sword shall enter into their own heart, and their bows shall be broken." It is another way of saying, "Whatsoever a man soweth, that shall he also reap" (Gal. 6:7).

In verses 16 to 20 you have the portion of the righteous, and you know God can take a very little that His dear people have and make it an abundance for them. "A little that a righteous man hath is better than the riches of many wicked." As long as you have a good conscience toward God and realize you are walking so as to please Him you can be happy, even though you are bereft of everything the worldling thinks he must have. Poor unsaved men have nothing but judgment ahead of them; but the children of the Lord have nothing but glory. "The Lord knoweth the days of the upright: and their inheritance shall be for ever. They shall not be ashamed in the evil time: and in the days of famine they shall be satisfied. But the wicked shall perish, and the enemies of the Lord shall be as the fat of lambs: they shall consume; into smoke shall they consume away."

In verses 21 to 29 you have the character of the righteous and the wicked again contrasted. Now let us see if we are not getting down to some rather serious things. What characterizes wicked people? Oh, you may say, cheating or lying or living immorally or getting drunk. Yes, but look at verse 21, "The wicked borroweth, and payeth not again: but the righteous sheweth mercy, and giveth." I am afraid there are a lot of people that God calls wicked that we have not been thinking of as wicked. There is something very practical here. God looks for practical righteousness between men and women, and dishonesty is characteristic of the wicked. Then look at the next verse, "For such as be blessed of Him shall inherit the earth; and they that be cursed of Him shall be cut off."

"The steps of a good man are ordered by the Lord: and He delighteth in his way." Somebody once picked up George Mueller's Bible and happened to be thumbing it over and came to this Psalm and noticed he had written something in the margin of verse 23. He found this, "The steps"—and in the margin he had written, *and the stops*— "of a good man are ordered by the Lord." Mr. Mueller had been meditating on it, and the thought came that it is not only the steps but also the stops that are ordered by the Lord. Sometimes you do not do any stepping; sometimes the Lord puts you on your back and says, "Now you glorify Me here." We can rest in the will of the Lord under all circumstances. "Though he fall, he shall not be utterly cast down: for the Lord upholdeth him with His hand."

And now David gives a lovely testimony. I know that temporal blessing was the promise of the Old Testament, and spiritual blessing is the promise of the New Testament; and very often the most devoted saints in this New Testament dispensation are left with very little of temporal blessing. On the other hand I am sure that where people learn to commit everything to God and walk in righteousness before Him, He is going to undertake for them. And so David's testimony is not without value to us. "I have been young, and now am old; yet have I not seen the righteous forsaken, nor his seed begging bread." Somebody may say, "Well, I do not like that because it makes me feel very bad. I have been in very difficult circumstances, and I have actually had to go and ask for help. I do not like to be put in the category of the wicked." This is not the case, for in our dispensation we do not have the same promise of temporal prosperity. But many of us fail to appropriate the privileges that are really ours in this age of grace. "Be [anxious] for nothing; but in every thing by prayer and supplication with thanksgiving let your requests be made known unto God" (Phil. 4:6). I believe that Christians would never have to beg for bread if they talked more to God. If we learned to depend on the living God and to go to Him, we would be amazed to find how He can undertake for us. God is the living God, and He will undertake if you will only trust Him. Is it not strange that we seem to be able to trust men more than we can trust Him? And yet we often get so disappointed in people, but we are never disappointed in Him if walking with Him. So David says, "I have been young, and now am old; yet have I not seen the righteous forsaken, nor his seed begging bread."

In verses 30 to 40 you have divine government In verse 34 we read, "Wait on the Lord, and keep His way, and He shall exalt thee to inherit the land: when the wicked are cut off, thou shalt see it." But the wicked seem to prosper in a way we do not. Yes, David says, they do: "I have seen the wicked in great power, and spreading himself like a green bay tree. Yet he passed away, and, lo, he was not: yea, I sought him, but he could not be found."

Now look at the contrast, "Mark the perfect man, and behold the upright: for the end of that man is peace." And so he closes the Psalm with these words, "The Lord shall help them, and deliver them: He shall deliver them from the wicked, and save them, because they trust in Him."

MAN'S FAILURE AND GOD'S GRACE
PSALMS 38 AND 39

PSALM 38 MIGHT BE DESIGNATED "THE PENITENT'S PLEA." It is the cry of a man who is distressed and broken-hearted because of his sin, and who comes to God acknowledging his guilt and looking to Him for forgiveness.

Over the first four verses we might write the word "Conviction." We have the expression here of a convicted soul, of a man who is not trying to make excuses for his sins. As long as you find a person endeavoring to excuse his sins and failures, you will know that the plowshare of conviction has never gone in deep enough. When King Saul was faced about his sin by Samuel he said, "I have sinned: yet honour me now, I pray Thee, before the elders of my people, and before Israel" (1 Sam. 15:30). In other words, Oh yes, I have done wrong, but make something of me in the eyes of the people. There is no evidence there of real conviction. When a man is truly convicted he stops making excuses and stops seeking honor for himself. And so in these four verses we listen to the Psalmist pouring out the feelings of his heart which is broken because of his sin.

"Oh Lord, rebuke me not in Thy wrath: neither chasten me in Thy hot displeasure. For Thine arrows stick fast in me, and Thy hand presseth me sore." What a mercy it is when one falls into sin—and such sin as David fell into—that God does undertake to deal with him, that the sharp arrows of the Almighty do pierce his soul, and that the hand of God is heavy upon him, making him feel the weight of his guilt. He continues, "There is no soundness in my flesh because of Thine anger; neither is there any rest in my bones because of my sin." He realizes he is righteously exposed to the anger of God. Sin demands punishment. We may try to excuse it, but God is "of purer eyes than to behold evil" (Hab. 1:13). God is never going to save one sinner and leave that sinner's sin unpunished. If He does not punish it on the sinner, it must be punished on the sinner's Substitute. And that is what took place on Calvary. At the Cross the Lord Jesus bore the judgment. The old hymn says,

> *"He bore on the tree the sentence for me,*
> *And now both the surety and sinner are free."*

"For mine iniquities are gone over mine head: as an heavy burden they are too heavy for me." It is the voice of a convicted sinner.

Over verses 5 to 14 we may write the word, "Humiliation." As he continues looking into his own heart, as he continues dwelling upon the sin that has crushed his life, he is bowed down before God in a sense of deepest humiliation. "My wounds stink and are corrupt because of my foolishness. I am troubled; I am bowed down greatly; I go mourning all the day long. For my loins are filled with a loathsome disease: and there is no soundness in my flesh. I am feeble and sore broken: I have roared by reason of the disquietness of my heart." Although feeling in his body and in his spirit the effects of his sin and knowing that God is dealing with him because of that sin, he realizes that there is no one else to whom he can turn for deliverance but to the very God that is afflicting him.

"Lord, all my desire is before Thee; and my groaning is not hid from Thee. My heart panteth, my strength faileth me: as for the light of mine eyes, it also is gone from me. My lovers and my friends stand aloof from my sore; and my kinsmen stand afar off." There is a sense in which the Lord Jesus entered into that. Though He was the absolutely holy One, when He took the sinner's place He could use such language as this. He could say, "My lovers and My friends stand aloof from My sore; and My kinsmen stand afar off. They also that seek after My life lay snares for Me: and they that seek My hurt speak mischievous things and imagine deceits all the day long." But now David, because he knew that he deserved what he was receiving, and Jesus, because He was taking our place and was accepting the judgment due to our sins as though He had deserved it, could use the words of the next two verses, "But I, as a deaf man, heard not; and I was as a dumb man that openeth not his mouth. Thus I was as a man that heareth not, and in whose mouth are no reproofs." It is a great thing to come to the place where you have no fault to find with anybody but yourself. Many of us spend so much of our time finding fault with other people. We can see other people's faults and can magnify their sins, but we are so unconscious of our own faults and sins. When people accuse us we get so indignant and forget that if our worst enemies knew all that we know about our own hearts and the sins of our own lives, they would say far worse than they do say. David here bows his head before God and has nothing to say because his own conscience is accusing him worse than any of them.

From the 15th to the 20th verse we have his confession. "For in Thee, O Lord, do I hope: Thou wilt hear, O Lord my God. For I said, Hear me, lest otherwise they should rejoice over me: when my foot slippeth, they magnify themselves against me. For I am ready to halt, and my sorrow is continually before me. For I will declare my iniquity,

I will be sorry for my sin." And you know what God says elsewhere, "He that covereth his sins shall not prosper: but whoso confesseth and forsaketh them shall have mercy" (Prov. 28:13). David says he will not try to cover it up, "I will declare my iniquity; I will be sorry for my sin. But mine enemies are lively, and they are strong: and they that hate me wrongfully are multiplied. They also that render evil for good are mine adversaries; because I follow the thing that good is." Once they blamed him for his sin; now they blame him for turning to God and professing to find in Him forgiveness.

In the last two verses he expresses his confidence, "Forsake me not, O Lord: O my God, be not far from me. Make haste to help me, O Lord my salvation."

Psalm 39 closes this series of fifteen Psalms by bringing before us in a very vivid way the contrast between human frailty and divine power, human sin and divine holiness. The first six verses seem to stand together and the Psalmist shows the utter emptiness of life without God. I trust that everyone of us realizes that. The old hymn is true:

> "I tried the broken cisterns, Lord,
> But ah, their waters failed.
> E'en as I stooped to drink they fled
> And mocked me as I wailed."

But at last the blessed Lord in grace took us up and we found the difference of the life in fellowship with God.

> "The pleasures lost I sadly mourned,
> But never wept for Thee,
> Till grace my sightless eyes received
> Thy loveliness to see.

> "Now none but Christ can satisfy,
> None other name for me;
> There's love and life and lasting joy,
> Lord Jesus, found in Thee."

So here we find this Old Testament believer—and it was David himself—learning the same lesson, the emptiness of life without God; and then the fullness of life when one knows God and lives in fellowship with Him. Look at those first six verses, "I said, I will take heed to my ways, that I sin not with my tongue: I will keep my mouth with a bridle, while the wicked is before me. I was dumb with silence, I held my peace, even from good; and my sorrow was stirred. My heart was hot within me; while I was musing the fire burned." God wants us to muse. To muse is to think, and God is seeking to get men to think. The prodigal never took a step toward his father until he sat down to think. We read, "He came to himself." The devil tries to keep people from musing, from thinking. Take that word so common today, "amusement." People are amusement crazy. The devil has all kinds of schemes to amuse people. Cut that word up, "Muse"—to think "A-muse"—not to think. The "A" there is the negative, and it simply means this, to stop thinking. That is why the theaters are crowded; that is why people love the dance; that is why people go to all these ungodly things of the world—to keep from thinking. If the devil can keep people from thinking, he will have them all doomed and damned eventually. But God wants us to think. His Word is a challenge to us to think.

David says, "I thought on my ways." Now he is musing, "Lord, make me to know mine end, and the measure of my days, what it is; that I may know how frail I am." It is a good thing to meditate along that line. People do not like to think of death; they do not like to think of an abrupt termination of life.

> "Life at best is very brief,
> Like the falling of a leaf,
> Like the binding of a sheaf,
> Be in time.
> Fairest flowers soon decay,
> Youth and beauty pass away,
> Oh, ye have not long to stay,
> Be in time."

People do not like to be reminded of the shortness of life David says, I sat down to think of it: how frail I am; how short a time I may have here, but I want my life to tell for the Lord; I want to do my very best for God. "Behold, Thou hast made my days as an handbreadth; and mine age is as nothing before Thee: verily every man at his best state is altogether vanity. Surely every man walketh in a vain shew: surely they are disquieted in vain: he heapeth up riches, and knoweth not who shall gather them." What a pitiable thing to have no hope beyond this life!

Beginning with verse 7 and going on to the end of the Psalm he changes to the other side of things and shows us that everything worth-while is found in God Himself. "And now, Lord, what wait I for? my hope is in Thee." I know that things of this world can never satisfy this poor heart of mine, but my hope, my confidence, and my trust are in Thee. "Deliver me from all my transgressions: make me not the reproach of the foolish. I was dumb, I opened not my mouth; because Thou didst it." When discipline came because of sin, he bowed his head and said, it is all right; it is the hand of God, and I deserve it. I accept it and trust it may be blessed to me, but if it please God to give deliverance, I will rejoice in His goodness.

"Remove Thy stroke away from me: I am consumed by the blow of Thine hand. When Thou with rebukes dost correct man for iniquity, Thou makest his beauty to consume away like a moth: surely every man is vanity. Hear my prayer, O Lord, and give ear unto my cry; hold not Thy peace at my tears: for I am a stranger with Thee, and a sojourner [a pilgrim]." I have only a little while to spend in this world, God help me to spend it for Thee, is what he is saying. Help me to live so that when I leave this scene behind I will realize it was well worth-while that I was permitted to glorify Thee when I was down in the world.

"O spare me, that I may recover strength, before I go hence, and be no more." That Hebrew expression translated, "spare me" is a significant one. Literally it might be rendered, "Look away from me, that I may recover strength." Do you remember in another place we read, "Look upon the face of Thine anointed," and so we link that with this, for as David realizes his own weakness, his own frailty, his own infirmity he exclaims, "Look away from me," for he sees that there is nothing in him to commend him to God. If thou, Lord, shouldest mark iniquities, O Lord, who shall stand?" (Psa. 130:3). There would be nothing but eternal judgment for me, but look away from me: look on the face of Thine anointed and accept me in Him. And that is exactly what God does. "He hath made us accepted in the Beloved" (Eph. 1:6).

THE PSALM OF THE BURNT OFFERING
PSALM 40

THE DEATH OF OUR LORD JESUS CHRIST IS PRESENTED IN different ways in Scripture. God, in type and shadow, has set it forth most marvelously in the first seven chapters of the book of Leviticus. There we read of five offerings: the burnt offering, the meal offering, the peace offering, the sin offering, and the trespass offering. These are all different but they all set forth various aspects of the Person and work of our Lord Jesus. The meal offering pictures His Humanity linked with His Deity. The peace offering presents Him as the One who made peace by the blood of His Cross. The sin offering shows us the sinless One made sin that we might become the righteousness of God in Him. The trespass offering tells us that Christ died for our sins, that He bore our sins in His own body on the tree. But the burnt offering presents in some respects the view of the work of the Cross that was more precious to God than all the rest, for it presents the Lord Jesus dying upon that Cross primarily in order that He might glorify God His Father in the scene where He had been so terribly dishonored by man's sin. The remarkable fact about all the other offerings is this: parts of them were presented on the altar and went up to God; other parts were divided among the people and the priests, and became the food of the people of God. But the whole burnt offering was placed on the altar and was all consumed: it all went up to God. He calls it, "My offering, My food." There was something in the sacrifice of our Lord Jesus Christ that no one could understand but God Himself. There was something about it that you and I could never enter into, could never appreciate in its fullness; there was something about it that God alone could enter into and appreciate.

This fortieth Psalm is really the Psalm of the burnt offering. The twenty-second is the Psalm of the sin offering, and that is the Psalm where we hear the Lord crying out, "My God, My God, why hast Thou forsaken Me?" (Psa. 22:1). The sixty-ninth is the Psalm of the trespass offering; and there we hear the Saviour exclaim from the Cross, "I restored that which I took not away" (verse 4). The eighty-fifth is the Psalm of the peace offering, and we read there, "Mercy and truth are met together; righteousness and peace have kissed each other" (verse 10). But in this fortieth Psalm we have the Lord Jesus presented as coming into the world and going to the Cross for the express purpose of doing the Father's will, and that is the burnt offering.

The first five verses tell of the depths of anguish into which He went and the deliverance that God gave Him. He says, "I waited patiently for the Lord; and He inclined unto Me, and heard My cry. He brought Me up also out of an horrible pit, out of the miry clay, and set My feet upon a rock, and established My goings." We take these words rightfully into our own lips, and we who are saved look back to the hole of the pit from which we were saved and sing sometimes, "He took me out of the pit and from the miry clay." Through grace we have a right to sing those words, but the pit in which we lay was as nothing to that into which He went in order that He might redeem us. He had to know infinitely more of the awfulness of sin and the horror of separation from God than you and I ever could possibly know. The most abject soul in the pit of woe will suffer only for his own sins, but our blessed Lord on the Cross bare the iniquity of us all. He had to drink to the full the cup of divine judgment against sin. The pit into which He sank was a horrible one indeed, but He came up again in triumph.

We hear Him say in verse 3, "And He hath put a new song in My mouth, even praise unto our God: many shall see it, and fear, and shall trust in the Lord." The new song is the song of redemption. Naturally when we read of a new song, the question arises in our minds, what is the old song? The old song is the song of creation. Away back in the book of Job we read, "Where wast thou when I laid the foundations of the earth?… when the morning stars sang together, and all the sons of God shouted for joy" (Job 38:4, 7). What a song that was when this world in all its pristine beauty sprang fresh from its Maker's hand and went circling off into space! Holy angels in rapture sang at the sight of it and all the hosts of God shouted for joy; but that song soon died away into a sad, bitter wail, for sin came in and blighted that fair creation, and God was dishonored in the universe that He had made. Then our Lord Jesus came and He went down into the depths into which sin had cast men in order that He might lift us out. He went to the Cross to glorify God who had been so terribly dishonored by man's sin and folly. And when He came forth from the tomb He was prepared to start the new creation singing. He leads the chorus. "He hath put a new song in My mouth, even praise unto our God." We read in the twenty-second Psalm, "In the midst of the congregation will I praise Thee" (verse 22).

> *"Join the singing that He leadeth,*
> *Now to God your voices raise;*
> *Every step that we have trodden*
> *Is a triumph of His grace."*

He is leader of the heavenly choir. When we turn to the book of The Revelation, where we get a sight into heaven itself, we see the elders gathered about the throne, and they sing a new song. It is a song of praise "unto Him who shed His blood to redeem us to God." Do you know that new song? No one will join in the new song over yonder and sing with the heavenly choir who has not learned the words down here. Unless you can say on earth, "Unto Him that loved us, and washed us from our sins in His own blood" (Rev. 1:5), you will never be able to sing it over there. We learn the song down here; we sing it here in our poor feeble way, but after "this poor lisping, stammering tongue lies silent in the grave," up yonder we shall sing as never before. When the resurrection of these bodies takes place and we gather about our great Choir Master in the glory how we will make the courts of heaven ring with this new song. And so our blessed Lord Jesus indicates what would be the blessed portion of those that trust Him, "Blessed is that man that maketh the Lord his trust, and respecteth not the proud, nor such as turn aside to lies." Then as He looks back to the depths of sorrow through which He went and sees how wonderfully God His Father has brought Him through, He exclaims, "Many, O Lord My God, are Thy wonderful works which Thou hast done, and Thy thoughts which are to us-ward: they cannot be reckoned up in order unto Thee: if I would declare and speak of them, they are more than can be numbered."

In verses 6 to 8 you have Him very definitely as the One who fulfills all these sacrificial shadows. Listen to Him speaking. "Sacrifice and offering Thou didst not desire; Mine ears hast Thou opened: burnt offering and sin offering hast Thou not required. Then said I, Lo, I come: in the volume of the book it is written of Me, I delight to do Thy will, O My God: yea, Thy law is within My heart." What is He really saying here? God had no real pleasure out of all those sacrifices and offerings under the law. Why? Because they could never put away sin. They were just figures, types, shadows. They bore practically the same relationship to the work of the Cross that a promissory note bears to the payment of a debt. It is getting the hard cash when the note falls due that gives one satisfaction. And so whenever an Israelite under law presented his offering, if he came as a repentant man to God in faith he was like a man giving his note to God acknowledging his indebtedness, and the Lord Jesus was the indorser of every note and said, as it were, "Some day I will settle them all." When He came to the earth and went to the Cross, He paid everything.

> "Jesus paid all my debt,
>   Oh wondrous love!
> Widest extremes He met,
>   Oh wondrous love.
> Justice is satisfied,
>   God now is glorified,
> Heaven's gate thrown open wide.
>   Oh wondrous love."

Sacrifices and offerings of old did not please the heart of God, but Jesus says, "Lo, I come"—I will go down into that world; I will become Man; I will become a Servant, and as a servant I am going to do the will of Him that sent Me; I will go to the Cross to do Thy will, O God, for "Thy law is within My heart." It is the burnt offering, the blessed Saviour going to Calvary to do the will of God. If not one soul were ever saved as a result of the work of the Cross, if everybody spurned it and rejected it, yet God has gotten more glory by the perfect obedience of His Son unto death than He ever lost by all of Adam's sin and all the sin that has come into the world since, because every sinner was but a finite creature but He who came to do the will of the Father is the infinite One. Our sin is finite but His obedience is infinite. At last One has been found to whom the will of God was the most precious thing in all the universe. We need to dwell on that side of it. We are apt to become too occupied with the work of the Cross for us. But God has been glorified in the work. And so in the seventeenth chapter of John, anticipating the Cross, we hear the Lord Jesus say, "I have glorified Thee on the earth: I have finished the work which Thou gavest Me to do" (verse 4).

And now the Psalm carries us on to the Resurrection. "I have preached righteousness in the great congregation: lo, I have not refrained My lips, O Lord, Thou knowest." God's righteousness has been sustained and maintained in the work of the Cross, and now the message of righteousness goes out to a lost world for that is what the gospel is—God's message to lost men telling them that the righteousness of God which once was against them is now for them. "I have not hid Thy righteousness within My heart; I have declared Thy faithfulness and Thy salvation: I have not concealed

Thy lovingkindness and Thy truth from the great congregation." And so, speaking to the Father as Man He can count on Him to bring all this to fruition.

"Withhold not thou Thy tender mercies from Me, O Lord." We think of Him again as the Man on His way to the Cross. "Let Thy loving kindness and Thy truth continually preserve Me. For innumerable evils have compassed Me about." Now notice this next expression, "Mine iniquities have taken hold upon Me, so that I am not able to look up; they are more than the hairs of Mine head: therefore My heart faileth Me." These words could not possibly be used by the Lord Jesus Christ because He had no iniquity, but He went into judgment and confessed our iniquities as His, and by refusing to speak, He was "brought as a lamb to the slaughter, and as a sheep before her shearers is dumb, so He openeth not His mouth" (Isa. 53:7). They laid to His charge things He knew not, but He had nothing to say, and they took silence for guilt. He stood there silent in the judgment and went to the Cross to bear our guilt, made our sins His own, and died for them in order that we might live. So He turns over everything to the hand of God. "Be pleased, O Lord, to deliver Me: O Lord, make haste to help Me. Let them be ashamed and confounded together that seek after My soul to destroy it; let them be driven backward and put to shame that wish Me evil. Let them be desolate for a reward of their shame that say unto Me, Aha, aha." That is, if men will not put their trust in the work of the Cross, there can be nothing but judgment for them. If they spurn the death of Jesus there is nothing but sorrow and desolation left. On the other hand, if men put their trust in Him, oh then, "Let all those that seek Thee rejoice and be glad in Thee: let such as love Thy salvation say continually, The Lord be magnified." Are you saying that? Are you able to say from the heart, "The Lord be magnified?" Paul says, "According to my earnest expectation and my hope, that in nothing I shall be ashamed, but that with all boldness, as always, so now also Christ shall be magnified in my body, whether it be by life, or by death" (Phil. 1:20).

But now we hear Messiah speaking once more as from the Cross just before He died, "But I am poor and needy; yet the Lord thinketh upon Me: Thou art My help and My deliverer, make no tarrying, O My God." How do you know that the Psalm refers to the Lord Jesus Christ? How do you know that it really presents Him as the Great Burnt Offering? Turn to Hebrews 10 and get the divine comment on this Psalm. The first verse, "For the law having a shadow of good things to come, and not the very image of the things, can never with those sacrifices which they offered year by year continually make the comers thereunto perfect. For then would they not have ceased to be offered? because that the worshippers once purged should have had no more conscience of sins." But there was not value enough in those sacrifices to purge a guilty conscience. "But in those sacrifices there is a remembrance again made of sins every year. For it is not possible that the blood of bulls and of goats should take away sins." But now listen, "Wherefore when He cometh into the world (and now you get the 40th Psalm), He saith, Sacrifice and offering Thou wouldest not, but a body hast Thou prepared Me: In burnt offerings and sacrifices for sin Thou hast had no pleasure. Then said I, Lo, I come (in the volume of the book it is written of me,) to do Thy will, O God. Above when He said, Sacrifice and offering and burnt offerings and offering for sin Thou wouldest not, neither hadst pleasure therein; which are offered by the law, Then said He, Lo, I come to do Thy will, O God. He taketh away the first [that is, the Old Testament sacrifices; He puts an end to them], that He may establish the second." His Cross stands eternally as the witness that God has been glorified and the sin question settled. "By the which will we are sanctified through the offering of the body of Jesus Christ once for all."

CONSIDERING THE POOR
PSALM 41

WE HAVE ALREADY NOTICED THAT THE BOOK OF PSALMS IS divided into five separate books. We come now to consider the last of this particular collection. We noticed that the first book of the Psalms is linked very intimately with the first book of the Pentateuch. It has to do with God as the Creator and Upholder of all things and as the Deliverer of His people, as the One who took us up in His electing love and having made us His own undertakes to carry us on in spite of all circumstances until at last we behold His face in righteousness. And everything hangs on the work of the Cross. As in the book of Genesis we have type after type setting forth the work of the Cross, so in this first part of the Psalms we have one Psalm after another that emphasizes the fact that every blessing for time and eternity comes to us through the work that our Lord Jesus Christ did when He took our place in judgment and was made sin for us upon the tree. That came out very clearly in Psalm 22 where we heard His anguished cry, "My God, My God, why hast Thou forsaken Me?" We saw it also in the fortieth Psalm where we looked upon the Lord Jesus as the burnt offering, presenting Himself without spot unto God, dying to glorify God in the scene where He had been so terribly dishonored by man's sin, and in glorifying God, working out salvation for us. We heard the voice of the Lord Himself speaking in that fortieth Psalm and noticed His cry in the closing verse, "I am poor and needy, yet the Lord thinketh upon Me: Thou art My help and My deliverer; make no tarrying, O My God." The One who uttered these words by the Spirit was really God over all blessed forevermore, who became Man in order that He might die for us. We read in 2 Corinthians 8:9, "For ye know the grace of our Lord Jesus Christ, that, though He was rich, yet for your sakes He became poor, that ye through His poverty might be rich."

We have noticed throughout this book that very frequently the last verse of one Psalm suggests the first thought of the one that follows it. And so we turn immediately to the first verses of the forty-first Psalm and read, "Blessed is he that considereth the poor: the Lord will deliver him in time of trouble." When we realize that the poor one here is our Lord Jesus Christ Himself, we can see the real force of these words. It is not so much that He is the poverty-stricken One; it is poor in the sense that one is weak and helpless, and that is what our Lord Jesus chose to become on the Cross. "He was crucified through weakness" (2 Cor. 13:4), we read. And this verse may be translated, "Blessed is he that thinketh upon the weakened one," the One who though He had all power and all might yet chose to be betrayed into the hands of sinners, refusing to exercise His divine omnipotence in order to deliver Himself, but was "brought as a lamb to the slaughter, and as a sheep before her shearers is dumb, so He openeth not His mouth" (Isa. 53:7). We can see how David typified Him.

The Psalm would suggest that it may have been written by David when he fled from Absalom, his son, when his own son turned against him and the great bulk of the army of Israel followed after Absalom. David left the city of Zion and passed over the brook Kedron, climbed the Mount of Olives, weeping, descended into the valley on the other side, and fled eventually across the Jordan. When his own son had turned against him, then he was indeed the poor one, the weakened one. You remember the story of Barzillai who heard of David's need and distress and came with all manner of fruit and provisions, and one can imagine David receiving these things with a grateful heart and sitting down to write this Psalm, "Blessed is he that considereth the poor: the Lord will deliver him in time of trouble." And of course the principle comes down to us. Do you want blessing yourself? Then be thoughtful and considerate of others who are in need. Do you know why some Christians, when they get in distress and trouble, cry to God and do not seem to get any answer? The reason often is this, when they were prosperous and others cried to them in their need and distress they did not give to them; they did not consider the poor, they did not minister to them, and the Lord says, as it were, Now you can just have a dose of your own medicine. You were not interested in others in the days of your prosperity; you were thinking of your own comfort; you knew that the poor and needy were all about you, and they pleaded in vain for help from you. So do not be surprised now if I turn you down. That is exactly what the Spirit of God intimates in the first Epistle of John when speaking of answers to prayer. The Lord has never promised to answer the prayer of one who is not walking in manifest love and concern for other people. Look at 1 John 3:16 to 22, "Hereby perceive we the love of God [Hereby know we love, R.V.], because He laid down His life for us: and we ought to lay down our lives for the brethren. But whoso hath this world's good, and seeth his brother have need, and shutteth up his bowels of compassion from him, how dwelleth the love of God in him? My little children, let us not love in word, neither in tongue; but in deed and in truth. And hereby we know that we are of the truth, and shall assure our hearts before Him.… If our heart condemn us not, then have we confidence toward God." If our own consciences tell us that we are indifferent to the needs of others in their distress, God is greater than our heart and knoweth all things. "Beloved, if our heart condemn us not"—if we know that we have walked before God with real concern for others, that we have not been living for self, then in our time of trial—"then have we confidence toward God. And whatsoever we ask, we receive of Him, because we keep His commandments, and do those things that are pleasing in His sight." This is the New Testament way of saying, "Blessed is he that considereth the poor: the Lord will deliver him in time of trouble."

J. Elder Cumming calls this Psalm The Sick Man's Cry," and as you read it you can realize that the writer was passing through a time of great physical stress. If he was not suffering from some actual disease, he was under a strain—his mind, and nervous system were under a terrible strain, but in the midst of it all he turned to God. Did you ever know what it was to be so tired and sick and nervous that it seemed you could not pray? That is a good time to use a prayer book. God has written some wonderful prayers for us in His own Word, and some of these we can use when we are so distracted and distressed that we do not know what to say ourselves. Many a time when so troubled I did not know how to pray or what to do I have sat down and read the Psalms and I would get hold of something that was the exact expression of my own personal need, and I have said, "Lord, this is Thine own Word, and this is the expression of my heart." Sometime when you are sick and nervous and tired and people do not understand you and everything is going wrong, sit down and take this forty-first Psalm and see if it does not make a wonderful prayer for you.

In the first three verses you will notice the Psalmist is really meditating; he is speaking about God and about what He will do for those who trust Him, but when he comes to verse 4 and down to the end of verse 12, he addresses the Lord directly. Let us notice his meditation. Verse 2, The Lord will preserve him, and keep him alive; and he shall be blessed upon the earth: and Thou wilt not deliver him unto the will of his enemies." Who? The one who considers the poor—first of all, the one who considers the poor Man, our blessed Lord Jesus Christ, and has put his trust in Him. But then the one who remembers the words of the Lord Jesus, "Ye have the poor with you always, and whensoever ye will ye may do them good" (Mark 14:7). I do not know any joy on earth like helping folk in their distress if they do not know who did it and then seeing how happy they are because of the help they get. I used to know a man in Sacramento, California, who was very wealthy and was always doing little things in a quiet way. He would find a Christian family in real distress, maybe in need of food, and he would go down to the grocer's and order such a splendid supply of things and then send it out to be delivered on the back porch with no explanation. The folk would come out and find the porch loaded with all these things and then would come to meeting and say, "Oh, the Lord did such a wonderful thing for me. I was in such need and did not know which way to turn, and then He sent me such a large supply of provisions." And that man would be so happy he would almost give away his secret and laugh out loud. Nothing gives more joy if you do it in a loving, Christlike, unostentatious way. Then when your day of trouble comes, and it is coming, do not think it is not, you can count on God to undertake for you.

"The Lord will preserve him, and keep him alive; and he shall be blessed upon the earth: and Thou wilt not deliver him unto the will of his enemies. The Lord will strengthen him upon the bed of languishing: Thou wilt make all his bed in his sickness." Is that not a wonderful thing when laid aside so weak you cannot rise, when you are confined to your bed with illness, to realize the Lord Himself is smoothing your pillow and freshening your covers? Think of the Lord making your bed for you. He will "make all his bed in his sickness." I have not been ill very much in my life but some of the greatest blessings I have had were when I was sick. I remember so well the first real sickness I had. I took typhoid fever and was sick for six weeks. I saw more as I lay there on my back looking up than I had seen for years walking around and looking down. The Lord made things more real and precious than I have ever known them to be in all the days going about in good health. And then I found that after I had been in that position I could help other people. I did not like to go to visit sick people before that. I would go to some poor sick one and would try to talk to him and I always felt that he thought, "What do you know about it? It is all right for you to tell me to trust the Lord and be patient, but you do not know anything about it." After that I could say, "I know all about it and know what the Lord can do for one in sickness." Some years before I had run across a little group of Christians in Idaho. A group of Swiss Christians had taken up large claims for farms, had cleared the forest and built their homes and raised their families. They built a chapel in the woods and as they came to service they would be singing in French as they rode down the river or as they came driving through the woods, and they filled the place. They loved the Word, but I could not speak French, and many of them could not talk English, so I would speak in English and one would interpret. They did not have a prayer meeting, and I talked to one of them about it and said, "I understand you do not have a prayer meeting."

"Oh," he said, "we come together to break bread in remembrance of the Lord, and for Bible study, but there is no need to come together to pray."

"Why not?" I asked.

"What do we have to pray for? We are blessed 'with all spiritual blessings in heavenly places in Christ' (Eph. 1:3), so we do not need to pray for more spiritual blessings. As for temporal blessings, the Lord knows what we need more than we do, and so we do not need to pray for temporal blessings. We do not have to pray for bigger farms for we have all the farms we can manage. We do not have to pray for children for I have nine and Brother So and So has thirteen. We do not need to pray for any of these things, so we do not have prayer meetings."

Well, I had a second attack of typhoid fever, and again I was looking up to heaven for six weeks, and when I got well enough to get home again I met this same brother, and he said, "We are so glad to see you. When we got word that you were down with typhoid fever again and were so far away from home, our hearts went out to you and we had prayer meetings, sometimes two or three times a week, praying for the Lord to raise you up again. Then we were so glad to hear that you were on your way back to California, and we haven't had any prayer meeting since."

I said, "I thank you for praying for me, but you know, when I was sick, I was having a wonderful time with the Lord. I need prayer more when I am strong and well than I do when sick."

When we come to verse 4 the Psalmist changes, and instead of speaking *about* the Lord, David speaks *to* the Lord. "I said, Lord, be merciful unto me: heal my soul; for I have sinned against Thee." There is nothing that exercises one like the trials that David went through. I am sure David had deep thoughts of heart when Absalom rebelled against him, when he had to flee from his presence; and I have an idea that David said to himself, "Oh, my son is treating me the way I treated God." David would not be able to forget those terrible failures that had come into his life, and he was suffering still under the hand of God because of them. Sin may be confessed, but after all, there are temporal consequences that follow. "Be not deceived; God is not mocked: for whatsoever a man soweth, that shall he also reap" (Gal. 6:7), and when David committed that awful sin that made such a blot upon his record you remember how he gave judgment against himself. Nathan came and told that story about the ewe lamb. David loved sheep and more than once he had put his life in jeopardy to save a lamb, and so when Nathan told of this rich man who took the ewe lamb and killed it in order to make a dinner for his visitors, he was wrought up and said, "The man that hath done this thing … shall restore the lamb fourfold" (2 Sam. 12:5, 6). And in this, David pronounced his own judgment. Nathan brought the word home to him and said, "Thou art the man." And David said, "I have sinned against the Lord." The Lord put away his sin, but there were temporal consequences still. David had said, "The man that hath done this thing … shall restore the lamb fourfold."

The little child that Bath-sheba bore took sick, and David went in and threw himself down before God and pled with the Lord to save that little child's life. By-and-by he noticed his servants whispering together, and he asked, "Is the child dead?" They said, "Yes." David went out and washed himself, sat down, and took food. "Why," they said, "what a strange thing! When the child was living you fasted and would not eat, and now the child is dead and you anoint yourself and eat." David said, "While the child was yet alive, I fasted and wept: for I said, Who can tell whether God will be gracious to me, that the child may live? But now he is dead … I shall go to him, but he shall not return to me" (2 Sam. 12:22, 23). There was David's first lamb taken away.

Then you remember how Amnon committed the very same kind of sin that his father had committed. It is an awful thing, "Visiting the iniquity of the fathers upon the children unto the third and fourth generation" (Ex. 20:5). The father goes into sin and the first thing you know the son goes into the same thing. And Absalom was so angry about the wrong wrought upon his sister that he slew Amnon. There was David's second lamb.

And then Absalom turned against his father, and this Psalm was written, perhaps, while David was fleeing from his presence. How David would have saved Absalom if he could. When Joab went out against Israel David said, "Deal gently for my sake with the young man, even with Absalom" (2 Sam. 18:5). But when Joab found him caught in the boughs of the tree, he drove three darts through his heart and David's third lamb had gone.

And now David is an old man, and Solomon has come to the throne, and it looks as though David is going to have to restore only threefold. But no, the last sorrow that he had was Adonijah, another son, who rebelled against Solomon and was put to death, and so David had restored fourfold. We need to realize that it is a serious thing to have to do with the living God. We get so careless about sin; we get so indifferent and imagine we can sin with impunity, but God's Book says, "Be sure your sin will find you out." David faces his sin and says, "I have sinned against Thee." He does not say, "Why do You call me to suffer like this?" No, he says, there is good reason for it for I have sinned. "If he have committed sins, they shall be forgiven him" (James 5:15). Then David speaks of enemies, and here we may realize how he becomes a type of the Lord Jesus Christ.

"Mine enemies speak evil of me, When shall he die, and his name perish?" That is the way they spoke of the Lord Jesus. "And if he come to see me, he speaketh vanity." Was that not like Judas coming to the Lord Jesus and saying, "Hail, Master," and kissing Him, pretending to be His friend? "His heart gathereth iniquity to itself; when he goeth abroad, he telleth it. All that hate me whisper together against me: against me do they devise my hurt." And then they are anxious to lay something on him. "An evil disease, say they, cleaveth fast unto him: and now that he lieth he shall rise up no more." In other words, now we have him where we want him. That is what they said when they crucified the Lord of glory but God raised Him from the dead.

And then in the ninth verse the reference is to Ahithophel the Gilonite, who had been David's friend. Do you know why he turned against him? Look up those names in the early chapters of Chronicles and you will make a remarkable discovery. Ahithophel was the grandfather of Bath-sheba. That is why he turned against David. David had wronged his granddaughter, and he betrayed David. Jesus had not wronged anybody, but Judas turned against Him, and the Lord uses these words about Judas, "Yea, Mine own familiar friend, in whom I trusted, which did eat of My bread, hath lifted up his heel against Me." Do you get the meaning of that expression? You have read it often. If it were translated into modern English it would be, "Mine own familiar friend, in whom I trusted, which did eat of My bread, hath kicked Me." You understand what it means to be disappointed in one you thought to be your friend, to have him turn against you and then kick you. If you have to suffer like that, go and talk it over with Jesus, for He has been through it all and

> "In every pang that rends the heat
> The Man of Sorrows hath a part."

In the next three verses David expresses his full confidence in God in spite of all that the enemies can do. "But Thou, O Lord, be merciful unto me, and raise me up, that I may requite them. By this I know that Thou favourest me, because mine enemy doth not triumph over me." He puts God between himself and the enemy. "And as for me, Thou upholdest me in mine integrity, and settest me before Thy face for ever." No one could say that like Jesus. Every one else must have certain reservations when using language like that, but the Lord Jesus could say it without any reservations whatever. "As for Me, Thou upholdest Me in Mine integrity, and settest Me before Thy face for ever."

The last verse not only closes the Psalm but it also closes this first book; and as we noticed on the first occasion that we examined the book of Psalms every one of the books ends with a doxology something like this, "Blessed be the Lord God of Israel from everlasting, and to everlasting. Amen, and Amen."

ABOUT CROSSREACH PUBLICATIONS

Thank you for choosing CrossReach Publications.

Hope. Inspiration. Trust.

These three words sum up the philosophy of why CrossReach Publications exist. To create inspiration for the present thus inspiring hope for the future, through trusted authors from previous generations.

We are *non-denominational* and *non-sectarian.* We appreciate and respect what every part of the body brings to the table and believe everyone has the right to study and come to their own conclusions. We aim to help facilitate that end.

We aspire to excellence. If we have not met your standards please contact us and let us know. We want you to feel satisfied with your product. Something for everyone. We publish quality books both in presentation and content from a wide variety of authors who span various doctrinal positions and traditions, on a wide variety of Christian topics that will teach, encourage, challenge, inspire and equip.

We're a family-based home-business. A husband and wife team raising 8 kids. If you have any questions or comments about our publications email us at:

ContactUs@CrossReach.net

Don't forget you can follow us on Facebook and Twitter, (links are on the copyright page above) to keep up to date on our newest titles and deals.

Bestselling Titles from CrossReach[1]

How to Be Filled with the Holy Spirit
A. W. Tozer

Before we deal with the question of how to be filled with the Holy Spirit, there are some matters which first have to be settled. As believers you have to get them out of the way, and right here is where the difficulty arises. I have been afraid that my listeners might have gotten the idea somewhere that I had a how-to-be-filled-with-the-Spirit-in-five-easy-lessons doctrine, which I could give you. If you can have any such vague ideas as that, I can only stand before you and say, "I am sorry"; because it isn't true; I can't give you such a course. There are some things, I say, that you have to get out of the way, settled.

God Still Speaks
A. W. Tozer

Tozer is as popular today as when he was living on the earth. He is respected right across the spectrum of Christianity, in circles that would disagree sharply with him doctrinally. Why is this? A. W. Tozer was a man who knew the voice of God. He shared this experience with every true child of God. With all those who are called by the grace of God to share in the mystical union that is possible with Him through His Son Jesus.

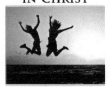

Tozer fought against much dryness and formality in his day. Considered a mighty man of God by most Evangelicals today, he was unconventional in his approach to spirituality and had no qualms about consulting everyone from Catholic Saints to German Protestant mystics for inspiration on how to experience God more fully.

Tozer, just like his Master, doesn't fit neatly into our theological boxes. He was a man after God's own heart and was willing to break the rules (man-made ones that is) to get there.

Here are two writings by Tozer that touch on the heart of this goal. Revelation is Not Enough and The Speaking Voice. A bonus chapter The Menace of the Religious Movie is included.

This is meat to sink your spiritual teeth into. Tozer's writings will show you the way to satisfy your spiritual hunger.

What We Are in Christ
E. W. Kenyon

I was surprised to find that the expressions "in Christ," "in whom," and "in Him" occur more than 130 times in the New Testament. This is the heart of the Revelation of Redemption given to Paul. Here is the secret of faith—faith that conquers, faith that moves mountains. Here is the secret of the Spirit's guiding us into all reality. The heart craves intimacy with the Lord Jesus and with the Father. This craving can now be satisfied.

Ephesians 1:7: "In whom we have our redemption through his blood, the remission of our trespasses according to the riches of his grace."

It is not a beggarly Redemption, but a real liberty in Christ that we have now. It is a Redemption by the God Who could say, "Let there be lights in the firmament of heaven," and cause the whole starry heavens to leap into being in a single instant. It is Omnipotence beyond human reason. This is where philosophy has never left a footprint.

[1] Buy from CrossReach Publications for quality and price. We have a full selection of titles in print and eBook. All available on Amazon and other online stores. You can see our full selection just by searching for CrossReach Publications in the search bar!

Claiming Our Rights
E. W. Kenyon

There is no excuse for the spiritual weakness and poverty of the Family of God when the wealth of Grace and Love of our great Father with His power and wisdom are all at our disposal. We are not coming to the Father as a tramp coming to the door begging for food; we come as sons not only claiming our legal rights but claiming the natural rights of a child that is begotten in love. No one can hinder us or question our right of approach to our Father.

Satan has Legal Rights over the sinner that God cannot dispute or challenge. He can sell them as slaves; he owns them, body, soul and spirit. But the moment we are born again... receive Eternal Life, the nature of God,—his legal dominion ends.

Christ is the Legal Head of the New Creation, or Family of God, and all the Authority that was given Him, He has given us: (Matthew 28:18), "All authority in heaven," the seat of authority, and "on earth," the place of execution of authority. He is "head over all things," the highest authority in the Universe, for the benefit of the Church which is His body.

The Two Babylons
Alexander Hislop

Fully Illustrated High Res. Images. Complete and Unabridged.

Expanded Seventh Edition. This is the first and only seventh edition available in a modern digital edition. Nothing is left out! New material not found in the first six editions!!! Available in eBook and paperback edition exclusively from CrossReach Publications.

"In his work on "The Two Babylons" Dr. Hislop has proven conclusively that all the idolatrous systems of the nations had their origin in what was founded by that mighty Rebel, the beginning of whose kingdom was Babel (Gen. 10:10)."—A. W. Pink, The Antichrist (1923)

There is this great difference between the works of men and the works of God, that the same minute and searching investigation, which displays the defects and imperfections of the one, brings out also the beauties of the other. If the most finely polished needle on which the art of man has been expended be subjected to a microscope, many inequalities, much roughness and clumsiness, will be seen. But if the microscope be brought to bear on the flowers of the field, no such result appears. Instead of their beauty diminishing, new beauties and still more delicate, that have escaped the naked eye, are forthwith discovered; beauties that make us appreciate, in a way which otherwise we could have had little conception of, the full force of the Lord's saying, "Consider the lilies of the field, how they grow; they toil not, neither do they spin: and yet I say unto you, That even Solomon, in all his glory, was not arrayed like one of these." The same law appears also in comparing the Word of God and the most finished productions of men. There are spots and blemishes in the most admired productions of human genius. But the more the Scriptures are searched, the more minutely they are studied, the more their perfection appears; new beauties are brought into light every day; and the discoveries of science, the researches of the learned, and the labours of infidels, all alike conspire to illustrate the wonderful harmony of all the parts, and the Divine beauty that clothes the whole. If this be the case with Scripture in general, it is especially the case with prophetic Scripture. As every spoke in the wheel of Providence revolves, the prophetic symbols start into still more bold and beautiful relief. This is very strikingly the case with the prophetic language that forms the groundwork and corner-stone of the present work. There never has been any difficulty in the mind of any enlightened Protestant in identifying the woman "sitting on seven mountains," and having on her forehead the name written, "Mystery, Babylon the Great," with the Roman apostacy.

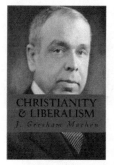

Christianity and Liberalism
J. Gresham Machen

The purpose of this book is not to decide the religious issue of the present day, but merely to present the issue as sharply and clearly as possible, in order that the reader may be aided in deciding it for himself. Presenting an issue sharply is indeed by no means a popular business at the present time; there are many who prefer to fight their intellectual battles in what Dr. Francis L. Patton has aptly called a "condition of low visibility." Clear-cut definition of terms in religious matters, bold facing of the logical implications of religious views, is by many persons regarded as an impious proceeding. May it not discourage contribution to mission boards? May it not hinder the progress of consolidation, and produce a poor showing in columns of Church statistics? But with such persons we cannot possibly bring ourselves to agree. Light may seem at times to be an impertinent intruder, but it is always beneficial in the end. The type of religion which rejoices in the pious sound of traditional phrases, regardless of their meanings, or shrinks from "controversial" matters, will never stand amid the shocks of life. In the sphere of religion, as in other spheres, the things about which men are agreed are apt to be the things that are least worth holding; the really important things are the things about which men will fight.

Elementary Geography
Charlotte Mason

This little book is confined to very simple "reading lessons upon the Form and Motions of the Earth, the Points of the Compass, the Meaning of a Map: Definitions."
It is hoped that these reading lessons may afford intelligent teaching, even in the hands of a young teacher.
Children should go through the book twice, and should, after the second reading, be able to answer any of the questions from memory.

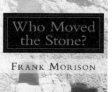

Who Moved the Stone?
Frank Morison

This study is in some ways so unusual and provocative that the writer thinks it desirable to state here very briefly how the book came to take its present form.
In one sense it could have taken no other, for it is essentially a confession, the inner story of a man who originally set out to write one kind of book and found himself compelled by the sheer force of circumstances to write another.
It is not that the facts themselves altered, for they are recorded imperishably in the monuments and in the pages of human history. But the interpretation to be put upon the facts underwent a change. Somehow the perspective shifted—not suddenly, as in a flash of insight or inspiration, but slowly, almost imperceptibly, by the very stubbornness of the facts themselves.
The book as it was originally planned was left high and dry, like those Thames barges when the great river goes out to meet the incoming sea. The writer discovered one day that not only could he no longer write the book as he had once conceived it, but that he would not if he could.
To tell the story of that change, and to give the reasons for it, is the main purpose of the following pages.

The Person and Work of the Holy Spirit
R. A. Torrey

Before one can correctly understand the work of the Holy Spirit, he must first of all know the Spirit Himself. A frequent source of error and fanaticism about the work of the Holy Spirit is the attempt to study and understand His work without first of all coming to know Him as a Person.

It is of the highest importance from the standpoint of worship that we decide whether the Holy Spirit is a Divine Person, worthy to receive our adoration, our faith, our love, and our entire surrender to Himself, or whether it is simply an influence emanating from God or a power or an illumination that God imparts to us. If the Holy Spirit is a person, and a Divine Person, and we do not know Him as such, then we are robbing a Divine Being of the worship and the faith and the love and the surrender to Himself which are His due.

In His Steps
Charles M. Sheldon

The sermon story, In His Steps, or "What Would Jesus Do?" was first written in the winter of 1896, and read by the author, a chapter at a time, to his Sunday evening congregation in the Central Congregational Church, Topeka, Kansas. It was then printed as a serial in The Advance (Chicago), and its reception by the readers of that paper was such that the publishers of The Advance made arrangements for its appearance in book form. It was their desire, in which the author heartily joined, that the story might reach as many readers as possible, hence succeeding editions of paper-covered volumes at a price within the reach of nearly all readers.

The story has been warmly and thoughtfully welcomed by Endeavor societies, temperance organizations, and Y. M. C. A. 's. It is the earnest prayer of the author that the book may go its way with a great blessing to the churches for the quickening of Christian discipleship, and the hastening of the Master's kingdom on earth.

Charles M. Sheldon.
Topeka, Kansas,
November, 1897.

Made in the USA
Thornton, CO
10/22/24 15:20:27

3f73ef6e-604c-4d42-a27a-ae7789f6eddbR01